PETER PRAN

JONATHAN WARD   TIMOTHY JOHNSON   PAUL DAVIS

essays
CHRISTIAN NORBERG-SCHULZ
KENNETH FRAMPTON
FUMIHIKO MAKI
JUHANI PALLASMAA
statement
DANIEL LIBESKIND

an architecture of poetic movement

altered perceptions

ANDREAS PAPADAKIS PUBLISHER

Telenor Headquarters

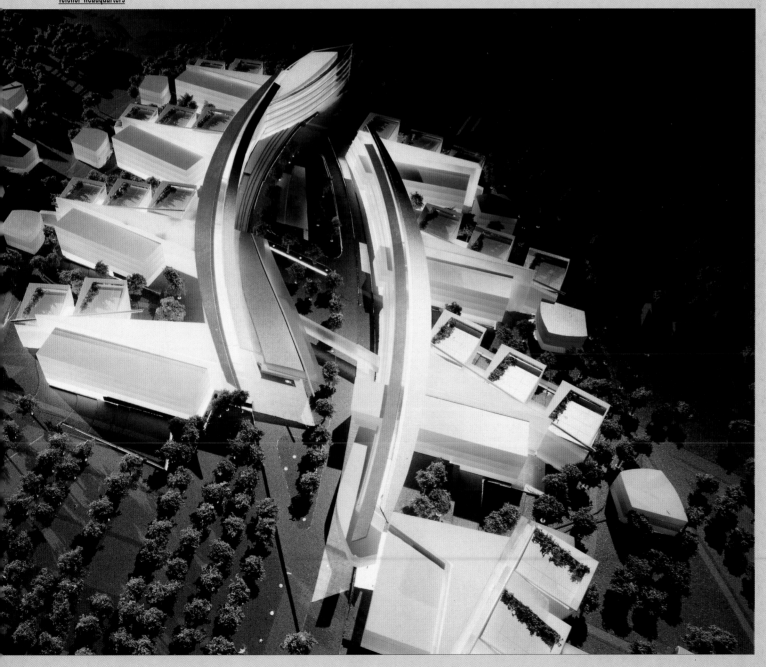

This book is dedicated to the memory of my wife Clevon Pran, for her love and compassion, and for her superb art that greatly influenced me – in my eternal love for her.

I wish first of all to express my profound gratitude to my publisher Andreas Papadakis for his strong belief in and support of my work, and for his initiation of and commitment to this new publication. My greatest thanks to Christian Norberg-Schulz, Kenneth Frampton, Fumihiko Maki, and Juhani Pallasmaa for their essays and to Daniel Libeskind for his statement. I am honoured by their words. My great appreciation to graphic designer Andrea Bettella. My high regards to my main assistant Joy Hale.

My most deep-felt thanks to those who have co-designed and collaborated closely with me on many of the thirty buildings and projects presented here: to Jonathan Ward, Timothy Johnson and Paul Davis for co-desiging with me for the last eight years on most of the buildings presented here, and for developing a strong, coherent design approach and language together with me over that time; to Carlos Zapata, who first co-designed and developed major concepts with me for six years until 1992 (from which period four projects/buildings are included here); and to Dorman Anderson, Joey Myers, Jin Ah Park, Jill Lerner, Dan Meis, John Gaunt, Wayne Fishback, Curtis Wagner, Maria Wilthew, Jim Jonassen, Bill Bain, Dave Hoedemaker, Scott Wyatt, Mike Hallmark, John Pangrazio, Ed Calma, Dave Koenen, Ron Turner, Ignatius Chau, Jeff Walden, Bill Nichols, Jim Waymire, John Savo, Phil Rubin, Ted McCagg, Jonathan Emmet, Mike Amaya, John Lodge, Michael Hootman, Mehrdad Yazdani, Mark Molen, Derek McCallum, Tim Carl, Joe Herrin, Friedl Bohm, Joe Rettenmeier, Guy Painchaud, Duncan Griffin, Alec Vassiliades, Diane Anderson, Susan Dewey, Allen Patrick, Rick Kuhn, Jordan Hukee, Leo Raymondo, Cece Haw, Lyn Rice, Steve McConnell, Rick Buckley, Frederick Norman, Tet Ogami, Vince Vergel de Dios, and Melissa Schrock, who developed major work with me.

I would further like to express my gratitude to those I have collaborated with on the architectural/ engineering/client teams outside my offices including Les Robertson, Saw-Teen See, Bill Faschan, Ron Klemencic, Dan Cornish, Tom Henry Knudsen, Tony Chi, Marvin Mass, Antonio Paulo Cordeiro, Richard Tenguerian, John Oldham, Bruce Fox, Norma Roca, Steven Papp, Skip Hommel, Jerry Kolb, Greg O'Connell, Bjorn Sorum, Lars Hauge, Jan Storing, Lois de Fleur, Suhadi Zaini, Michael Fieldman, Gene Kimm, Young-Jae Lee, Brian Curtner, David Han, Michio Sugawara, Hideto Takanaka, Joe Colaco, Rahmat Ismail, Claudette Weber, Abraham Razack, Jon Magnusson, Charlie Anderson, David Levin, and Virginio Ferrari.

From my very important years as an architect in Chicago, of those I worked with, my gratitude extends most of all to Myron Goldsmith, Gene Summers, Mies van der Rohe, Fazlur Khan, Bruce Graham, David Sharpe, Pao-Chi Chang, Peter Carter, Phyllis Lambert, Bruno Conterato, Daniel Brenner, George Danforth, Mike Pado, Oswald Grube, and Franz Schulze.

I am very grateful to the NBBJ partners and principals who have fully supported the publication of this book.

I would also like to thank all those too numerous to mention whom I have known or know and admire and who have had a major influence on my work.

Peter Pran

First published in Great Britain in 1998 by
Andreas Papadakis Publisher
an imprint of Cranbourne Investments International Limited,
Kilbees Farm, Hatchet Lane, Windsor, Berks SL4 2EH

ISBN 1 901092 07 0 pb
ISBN 1 901092 08 9 hb

Printed and bound in Singapore

Contents

The Return to Modernism
Christian Norberg-Schulz

During the last decade the return to modernism has become an urgent need. I say "need" because a new start was imperative after the failure of post-modernism. Habermas's characterization of modern architecture as an "unfinished project"[1] implied an invitation to proceed from where modernism seemingly got stuck after World War II. But *how* to get on was anything but clear. Does a new start mean to exploit the unused potential of early currents such as neo-plasticism or constructivism, or does it demand entirely new inventions? Both possibilities have come to the fore during the last decade. Richard Meier is the most obvious representative of the first alternative, whereas Frank Gehry stands forth as the inventor of things unknown. But do they and the rest of the avant garde really tell us how architecture ought to be today?

Peter Pran is one of those who aim at reviving modernism. He explicitly defines himself a "modernist," and states that he certainly is not a deconstructionist.[2] The purpose of this book is to illustrate his present endeavour and also to judge how his work is related to the original aims of modern architecture. First of all, the book gives testimony to an extraordinary creative output; not many architects of today may compete with Pran on number of significant large-scale projects.

Pran himself characterizes his work as an "architecture of poetic movement," and movement is indeed a quality common to all his later works. In this sense, he certainly is a "modernist," since modern architecture from the very beginning was distinguished by an outspoken dynamism.[3] As to their poetic content, I may mention that Pran's high-rise buildings are inspired by Brancusi's *birds*, and that he in general aims at realizing a preciseness akin to the works of the great Romanian sculptor. To be able to evaluate Pran's achievement, it is, however, necessary to take a look at the ends and means of modern architecture.

It is a deplorable fact that modern architecture over and over again is attacked for being a manifestation of mere rationalism, with the aim of arriving at a unitary and generally valid world view. Hence modernism is by many considered authoritarian and even totalitarian.[4] This criticism is unfair, because it stems from

basic misunderstandings, and also blocks our access to its real value. It is certainly true that the protagonists of modern architecture felt a strong attraction to reason and technology, but it is equally true that their goal was an architecture of poetic quality. Le Corbusier's statements in *Vers une architecture* (1923) are well known and do not have to be repeated here (although they seem to be "forgotten" by his critics). Let me instead recall Gropius's words in *The New Architecture and the Bauhaus* (1935): "... rationalization, which many people believe to be its cardinal principle, is really only its purifying agent. ... The other, the aesthetic satisfaction of the human soul, is just as important as the material."[5] Even the most austere of the early protagonists, Mies van der Rohe, in the preface to the Weissenhof-catalogue defined the creation of a new dwelling as *eine baukünstlerische Aufgabe*.[6] Let me conclude that modernism was an *artistic* movement, and buildings such as the Villa Savoye, the Barcelona Pavilion and the Bauhaus may serve as proofs.

Why, then, do so many want to reduce modern architecture to a mere question of "function" and "economy?"[7] Have they not read the original texts, or are they distorting the facts in order to make their own inventions more plausible? Perhaps the main reason is that the true nature of modernism has never been adequately explained.[8]

The most explicit statement about the deeper aims of modernism is due to S. Giedion: "Contemporary architecture had to take the hard way. As with painting and sculpture it had to begin anew. It had to reconquer the most primitive things, as if nothing had ever been done before."[9] Giedion here says that to "begin anew" means to "reconquer the most primitive things," that is, to return to the origins, forgetting everything that had been done throughout history. It would, however, be a misunderstanding to interpret his words as a demand for essentialism and a unitary world view. And this is precisely the misunderstanding from which the attacks on modernism stem. To "reconquer the most primitive things" is not an *exclusive* endeavour, to quote Venturi's word, but rather an *inclusive* one, since what is primitive or original, is open to an infinitude of interpretations, and in this sense "includes" everything that is to come. Louis Kahn understood that when he said: "In the start lies the seed for all things that must follow."[10] To "forget" history therefore does not imply that we should not learn from it, but that we should avoid to be dependent on stylistic preconceptions and models. History teaches us what interpretation of the origins means. Thus it illustrates the embodiment of *principles*, a world that in fact means "beginnings." In this context I may recall Vincent Scully's words: "The impression becomes inescapable that in Kahn, as with Wright, architecture began anew."[11] Modern architecture, thus, did not die after World War II; many architects such as the members of Team X remained faithful to its aims, and it is an interesting fact that Kahn himself presented his ideas for the first time at the Team X conference in Oterlo 1959.[12] Before I return to the role of Peter Pran in the more recent development of modernism, it is, however, necessary to say a few words about its means.

From the beginning, modern or rather pre-modern architecture was distinguished by a new conception of space. Numerous early writers on the subject, such as van Doesburg and Moholy-Nagy stress this fact, which was synthesized by Le Corbusier in his term *plan libre*.[13] It is important to realize that the word *libre* does not imply arbitrary freedom, but a space that "flows" between elements of varying definition and stability. Thus Mies van der Rohe's Barcelona Pavilion distinguishes between zones of diverse dynamism, and in a new sense between outside and inside. The famous onyx-wall, for instance, is a manifestation of "inside," and would be meaningless at the periphery of the composition. The "free plan" may therefore be understood as a "system of interacting places," and on this basis it became subject to a significant development after World War II.[14] The free plan is necessarily linked with the "free facade" and the "free partition." That is, what in the past were understood as parts of a stylistic system, now are expressive in their own right; they become what Le Corbusier called *objets de réaction poétique*. Hence they make a return to the origins manifest, just like the "elements" employed by painters such as Kandinsky, Klee and Mondrian.

Let us on this background take a closer look at Pran's works. After graduating from the Oslo School of Architecture in 1961, he went to Chicago where he got a master's degree at the Illinois Institute of Technology in 1969. In the meantime he was employed as an architect and project designer by Mies van der Rohe (1963-66) and Skidmore, Owings and Merrill (1966-69). Thus he had the occasion to work on significant projects such as the National Gallery, Berlin (1963), the Chicago Federal Center (1965), the Toronto Dominion Center (1966) and the Sears Tower (1968). On the basis of these experiences, Pran published in 1968 and 1971 two articles in the Norwegian professional magazine *Byggekunst*, the first on high-rise structures, with Chicago's John Hancock Building as the main example, and the second on wide-span halls, using a project of his own as an illustration.[15] The choice of topics is significant since both are at the roots of modern architecture. The iron-and-glass buildings of the nineteenth century, thus, introduced the wide-span hall and the "skyscraper" as main expressions of the new conception of space. London's Crystal Palace realized the hall theme already in 1851, and it was followed by Horeau's great project for an exhibition hall (1867) and the *Galerie des machines* for the Paris fair in 1889. The "rise of the skyscraper" took place in Chicago and was initiated by William Le Baron Jenney after the great fire in 1871.[16] Since then the two themes have been central to the development of modern architecture, and in particular to Mies van der Rohe, whose Crown Hall at the IIT had just been finished when Pran arrived in Chicago, whereas the 860 Lake Shore Drive apartment towers had been up since 1951. Undoubtedly, Mies van der Rohe remains the strongest source of inspiration for Pran, not to say the only one,. Pran has in fact pursued high-rise and wide-span structures throughout his career, and in this sense he is a true "modernist." But his recent projects do not have the orthogonal order of Mies's later designs. Rather they develop possibilities inherent in his early projects for Friedrichstrasse in Berlin. When I once asked Mies why he made no use of curves, he answered: "The Baroque architects were able to do that, but they were the result of a long evolution."[17]

This evolution becomes manifest in the later works of Peter Pran. When he himself calls his designs "an architecture of poetic movement," it implies that the spatial flow is no longer a mere manifestation of openness and interaction, but has become a subtle expression of the transformations present in the late-modern field of spatial forces. Pran's high-rise buildings are usually split into two vertical slabs, one which is orthogonal and one which is curved and warped.[18] The first expresses the basic role of gravitation in architecture, whereas the other makes the rising up in space a "flight," which, as already mentioned, he relates to Brancusi's birds. Even the warped slab, however, remains clearly defined and regular. Between the two, and other volumes on the ground, the spaces of circulation are truly dynamic. Here, the "free plan" has become an expression of the complex and often contradictory life on earth, whereby the rising "bird" gains a liberating effect. In fact Kenneth Frampton says that "Pran's architecture seems to intend a modernity that is liberative."[19]

Peter Pran's recent hall-projects are equally dynamic. Of particular interest is his prize-winning design for the Seoul World Football Championship Stadium for 2002 (project 1997), which is a multi-use space for baseball, soccer, American football, concerts and exhibits. Again a series of distinct volumes are interrelated by intermediate spaces of circulation, making up a "free plan" of large dimensions.

Among Pran's later works, two stand out as particularly evident manifestations of the *return to modernism*: the New York State Psychiatric Institute and the New York Police Academy, both from 1992. With their combination of orthogonal and curved units, both plans secure spatial adaptation to the New York grid as well as the flow of parimetral freeways. Basic traits of the modern "language" of forms are combined in a way that is simultaneously rational and expressive. A certain wish for simplification is evident, which shows that Pran, after all, grew up with Mies's dictum "less is more." Furthermore the solutions remind us of Giedion's understanding of the "undulating wall" as the original manifestation of the new conception of space. In Pran's works curvature acts horizontally as well as vertically, whereby

spatial dynamism becomes comprehensive, without however contradicting the fundamental dichotomy of down and up, which so often happens in deconstructivist works.

With his prize-winning project for the Telenor headquarters in Oslo, Pran has furthermore demonstrated how the undulating wall may serve to create a new kind of dominant urban space; a space that brings back life to the extended grid patterns of corporate lay-outs.

Because of their inherent quality of poetic movement, Pran's high-rise structures may act as true urban *centres*. They do not primarily express their functional content, but serve to *gather* the late-modern field of unrelated units. Pran's visions of expressive verticality thus show us that the "unfinished project" of modernism is gaining a new significant dimension.

1 J. Habermas, *Der philosophische Diskurs der Moderne*, Frankfurt a.M., 1985.

2 Personal information.

3 C. Norberg-Schulz, *Roots of Modern Architecture*, Tokyo, 1988.

4 O. Maystad, "Modernisme og terrorisme," *Arkitektnytt*, Oslo, 1992.

5 W. Gropius, *The New Architecture and the Bauhaus*, London, 1935, p. 23.

6 L. Mies van der Rohe, *Bau und Wohnung*, Stuttgart, 1927.

7 H. Meyer, *Bauen und Gesellschaft*, Dresden, 1980.

8 An attempt is made in Norberg-Schulz, *op. cit.*

9 S. Giedion, *Architecture You and Me*, Cambridge, Mass., 1958, p. 26.

10 O. Newman, *CIAM '59 in Otterlo*, Stuttgart, 1961, p. 207.

11 V. Scully, *Louis I. Kahn*, New York, 1962, p. 25.

12 Newman, *op. cit.*, pp. 205ff.

13 The concept was defined about 1976.

14 For instance in the early works of Paolo Portoghesi. See C. Norberg-Schulz, *On the Search for Lost Architecture*, Rome, 1975.

15 P. Pran, *Byggekunst*, Oslo, 1968; *Byggekunst*, Oslo, 1971.

16 C. Condit, *The Rise of the Skyscraper*, Chicago.

17 C. Norberg-Schulz, "Rencontre avec Mies van der Rohe," *L'Architecture d'aujourd'hui*, 79, 1958.

18 For instance in the Bin Laden Headquarters in Jeddah, 1990; and the De Centrale Lokatie, The Hague, Netherlands, 1992.

19 *op. cit.*, pp. 10ff.

An Architecture for an Age of Complexity and Change
Fumihiko Maki

Cubism and De Stijl were perhaps the first artistic movements that recognized the visual complexity of our world; by registering our altered perception of the visible world, those artists gave birth to a new conception of modernity. Today, nearly a century after the emergence of the artistic avant-garde, we still find ourselves in search of modernity, an ideal whose essence lies in the quest of defining what and where we are now. The task shows little sign of exhausting itself, for the ever-changing present seems to be an inherently undefinable condition.

The technological advances and the coming together of cultures during our times have greatly expanded our ability to see, hear, analyze, and communicate the complexity of our world. Our increased awareness of this complexity allows us more than ever to perceive intricate relations between the trivial actions of everyday life and the global issues society faces. Thus our materialistic desire for higher living standards is now seen in the context of the need to conserve natural resources; our pursuit of larger economic networks, in the context of maintaining smaller ethnic and cultural identities; our aspiration for excellence, in the context of an egalitarian faith in the common good for the common man. Modernity thrives on conflict, dilemma, and irony, which continuously challenge our curiosity and capacity to reason.

Within this intellectual climate, it is not difficult to see in each of the myriad artistic works being produced today an intentional response to this notion of complexity. This may be particularly true in the field of architecture, an art whose functional grounding has historically required a high level of synthesis of complex goals. Today the architect is regularly asked to make sense of an ever-increasing list of programmatic requirements and performance expectations, and the creation of good architectural space at times requires a nearly superhuman effort to overcome the trivial and the tangential. Some designers address the issue of complexity by simple denial — in this sense, the minimalist aesthetic makes a strong commentary on our times. Others choose instead to take advantage of the very energy of complexity — for them, the overlapping, contradictory conditions of our times provoke a saturated visual response based on sensual collage.

The work of Peter Pran belongs to this second school, the school of complexity — in fact, he might be called one of the school's foremost advocates. Pran's design builds on a fragmentary aesthetic of floating planar elements that seem to deny gravity and blur distinctions between inside and outside space — in this, he makes use of the legacy of De Stijl's compositional principles. Yet his formal vocabulary is far richer than the sober orthogonal world of those earlier Dutch modernists — in particular, his use of curved surfaces in close juxtaposition to orthogonal lines creates considerable tension within and between spaces. The contrast of straight and curved lines, rather than merely the curve itself, is responsible for the richness of visual and spatial experience in his projects. The sensual abandon with which Pran shapes spaces of passage and points of juncture lends the entire spatial composition a strong sense of fluidity and movement. Yet there is a high degree of control, precision and logic that determines these curves; one never senses that his architecture has left the realm of rational constructs.

Pran's strong compositional moves end up serving more than merely visual ends. The visual energy of his designs disarms the conventional prescription of human activity of prosaic programmes. Unusual spaces and unexpected scenes allow us to reinterpret programmes as we see new spatial relationships emerging; the relationship between form and function thus becomes a reciprocal process of criticism, rather than a linear means of determining design.

In many ways, architectural design has always involved this process of trial and error. Design entails never-ending cycles of production, criticism, and refinement. It is only the restraints of time and energy that circumscribe this process. Peter Pran has found that the computer has proved to be an invaluable tool in facilitating faster cycles:

"The computer has allowed us to open up a new world of three-dimensional plasticity, richness, and complexity. ... We can now explore the forms, spaces, and connections in a facile real-time mode in which we can make better and faster decisions. ... These understandings that are so fundamental to architecture, but are often abstracted to the level of absurdity in the traditional design process, must be captured in this architecture."

The computer has thereby initiated a new design mentality of which Peter Pran stands at the forefront. This "feedback" process of creating architecture manifests itself in an increased complexity of forms; spatial conditions arise that could not have been visualized before the advent of the computer.

Since architecture in the end is always a social art, one could say that the visual aspect of architecture reflects to some degree social behaviour. The interest in novelty that characterizes modernism might simply derive from a desire to see evidence of underlying behavioural change. If this is so, then we might look to Pran's fluid, discontinuous compositions to perceive a certain breakdown in conventional notions of formal hierarchy. Traditionally, the classic architectural approach was to divide given spaces into served and servant spaces; typically this translates into a distinction between rooms of specific function (served space) and corridors linking them (serving space). But today, the corridor, the place of movement, has become more important for daily use, and in an effort to accommodate this change, traditional distinctions between serving and served spaces have been blurred forever. Pran's designs concentrate their greatest impact on these territories of public passage, using curved surfaces to impart an expansiveness and natural dignity to this "servant" space. His designs inevitably treat the idea of passage as an episodic, fragmentary experience, and this fragmentary aesthetic leads him freely to a multi-centred organization of programme wholly suited to the complex programmes he tackles. More than being mere visual excitement, however, Pran's energetic proposals for orchestrating buildings around the space of public passage point to a real need for a more creative exploration of the programme by today's architects and clients.

I am told that this volume will stand as a testament to Pran's relationship to modernism. The modern era has been characterized by a world constantly increasing in complexity and an implicit human will to understand that world rationally. Paradoxi-

cally, the computer has played an integral role in reinforcing both these criteria. From the universe to the micro-organism, computers have provided rational insight into every aspect of human life. At the same time, they have uncovered parts of the world for which humans would never have thought to look. Computers have thereby facilitated a rational understanding of the world while continually increasing that world's perceived complexity. This paradox actually moves humans that much further away from rationally understanding what and where we are now.

One can view Pran's relation to modernism and the computer in much the same way. Using the computer as a design tool, Pran has been able to represent unbuilt architecture with unprecedented accuracy. The building and its spaces are rationally determined before they are built, and this enables him to experiment with more complex forms. The resulting increase in complexity uncovers new relationships among the elements, invigorating the architecture with interest, vibrancy, and life. In the course of uncovering new formal relationships, new programmatic and human relationships are manifested, and the process of rationally understanding these phenomena begins anew.

Just as architectural design is a feedback process, so too is the course of modernism. Human thought and activity influence the built environment, which, in turn, influences human thought and activity. Pran himself states that a goal of architecture is to "offer a perception of life and art and our place in the world which is perhaps unknown or unthought of." By offering something new, Pran is at once commenting on and changing the present — one of the infinite "feedbacks" inherent to modern life. Kinetic, fragmentary, and cinematic, his designs seem to capture something essential about the spirit of this age of complexity and change. As our cyclical age spirals incessantly into the next millennium, Peter Pran seems to be one of the few architects up to the challenge of executing this kind of exciting work convincingly in both large and small scale, as a number of recent projects by his deft hand will attest. In an age of intellectual controversy and irony, the poetry of his forms has the ability to silence words and remind us of the ineffable.

A Continuing Experiment: Peter Pran in NBBJ
Kenneth Frampton

"Are not mistakes in judgment natural? For is criticism so easy?
Is not true criticism as rare as art?"
Ludwig Mies van der Rohe, *Das Kunstblatt*, 1930

Peter Pran is a unique figure who has been able to sustain an informal design collaborative as he has shifted his operations from one corporate practice to another. In his move from Ellerbe Beckett to NBBJ, he has been able to carry with him many of the young architects with whom he has been involved on a wide range of projects over the past decade. What this effort has meant to the younger generation has been well accounted for by his colleague Jonathan Ward:

"The work that is represented here is the work of a collaborative — not a collective — and certainly not the usual architectural dictatorship. It is an attempt to move away from the typical modes of either the corporate firm or the small iconoclast firm and define a different way of working that results in a unique product. The collaborative is by definition ephemeral and ever-changing, depending on the desires of individuals involved at any given time. ... The leadership of the design vision and the direction of the practice must be clear and focused; otherwise the architecture and the livelihood of the firm will become compromised."[1]

Despite the disruption of having to shift his base of operations Pran has maintained a consistent line — that unique Neo-Constructivist vision with which he has been able to sustain the enthusiasm of his team. This has been sustained in a period that has seen major changes in the nature of American corporate practice, first because of the introduction of digital technology and, second, in part, because of the play of the global market, as American architects have turned first this way and then that in search of a new client base. In the light of these circumstances we may identify three consecutive phases in Pran's recent practice: first, four major works designed for New York State and New York City, most of which are either built or close to completion; second, a series of ambitious proposals for Hong Kong, China, Indonesia, Korea, the Philippines and Brazil, and last, a number of current corporate designs in Europe and the United States, including the Telenor Headquarters to be built in Oslo, Norway, and the Vulcan Headquarters Building to be built, significantly enough, for Paul Allen.

In each of these phases the commissions have been for different classes of clientele, each having its own distinct demands and expectations, not to mention the varying technological capacity that is to be found from one aspect of the global economy to another. Thus, in New York State the Pran team would encounter the programmatic stability of the state, subject to the economic constraints of the late-modern, American public client, while in South East Asia they would find themselves confronted by private clients in overheated economies, mostly aspiring to the futuristic imagery irrespective of the limitations of the local building industry and their undue dependence on the importation of expensive materials and techniques.

These contradictions in the field have been accompanied by other fundamental changes, not only the shift to computer aided design but also the increasing impatience of the private client who seems to lack the ability to allow the design to evolve at a reasonable pace and invariably wishes to have every issue resolved overnight. In this regard recent transformations in the nature of the design process have perhaps engendered as many losses as gains, for while physical modelling remains an integral part of the design process, today's clients have developed an insatiable appetite for rapid seductive images to be generated through computer modelling particularly since they appear to represent with photographic authority the building as it will be seen on completion. While the computer facilitates the rapid graphic modification of details the advantages of the average CAD system have been offset, to some extent, by a growing reluctance, due to a lack of time, to build accurate models at a sufficiently detailed level. It is as though the facility of one forecloses upon the palpability of the other. Thus, the full three-dimensional consequences of a work often remain underexamined and, at the same time, the material vision of the architect fails to find analogous expression in the various materials from which the model is made. For client and architect alike, crucial decisions are based on a computer image instead of being derived from the more tactile, spatial information offered by a model. This escalation in the speed of decision-making tends to favour the perspectival rendering rather than the physically modelled work by which one may simulate, in a more definitive way, the penultimate co-ordinates of a particular profile or section. Many of these difficulties have been overcome at the NBBJ practice in part, ironically enough, through the use of Silicon Graphics hardware and Alias/Wavefront 3D visualization software. Nevertheless, despite the digital tendency, the Pran team is still dedicated to the building of detailed models in order to complement their mastery of CAD.

At the same time, one knows that no form of rendering is neutral and that this is as true of computer drawing as any other media. We can see an example of original computer images made for Pran's SUNY Academic Building in Binghamton where the symbolic entry between the opposing wings of the complex was initially envisaged as a delicate interplay between opposing transparent prisms. As it happened, this could not be fully realized, owing to the New York State building code that stipulates the use of tinted rather than clear glass. However, this lost transparency reappears at night when the building is artificially lit. And yet, irrespective of this perceptual compromise, it is clear that SUNY Binghamton represents a major departure from what has been standard New York State building practice, particularly of recent date, and for this, credit has to be accorded not only to Pran, but also to the client, Lois de Fleur, the president of SUNY.

The New York State Psychiatric Institute[2] in Manhattan is an equally remarkable solution to the task of providing a complex medical facility in an interstitial green space between the Westside Highway and Riverside Drive. Here once again, the client, the director of the Institute, Dr. John Oldham, played a crucial role in navigating his way through the bureaucratic labyrinth that invariably serves to undermine such daring proposals. However, the core of this exceptional building has been somewhat compromised by the over-structuring of its six-storey glazed atrium, once again testifying to the fact that visionary architects need to be matched by equally visionary engineers. Even if the tilted structural span of 120ft remains impressive in its own terms, the structure of the trussed girders of the six-storey curtain wall is by no

means as elegant as the engineering of the two bridges that span the roadway between the base hospital and the institute.

Pran's expressionist Neo-Constructivist approach assumes a more typological character in the New York Police Academy, designed in association with Michael Fieldman and Partners.[3] This is suggested by the formative role played by the running track in the overall design, the symmetry of which was used to establish the axis about which the muster deck is planned. At the same time, in contrast to the regularity of the track, the sweeping classroom block, progressively rising in height from one end to the other, is surely a didactic example of Pran's "topography of movement." A similar, if less dramatic, Mendelsohnian expression is evident in the NYCT Rail Control Center,[4] now nearing completion in Manhattan. Here, despite the strict orthogonal plan dictated by the site, the energetic linearity of the facade is assured by horizontal metal panelling and by a contrasting stone-faced Neoplastic composition at one end of the frontage.

Sports buildings have been a strong theme in Pran's work ever since the McCormick Place Stadium projected for Chicago in 1990. In 1997, Pran, in collaboration with Dan Meis of the NBBJ/LA office, designed the Lucky Goldstar Seoul Dome Stadium in Seoul, Korea which was won in a limited competition against Toyo Ito, Nicholas Grimshaw, and Helmut Jahn. In this design a 70,000 seat arena finds itself enclosed by bands of entertainment and other mixed use accommodation.[5] This audacious proposal (which must be completed for the World Cup of 2002) turns on the notion that football fans may be conveniently distracted both before and after the match by a wide variety of *flaneur* entertainment, including restaurants, health-spas, and shops together with a large number of "cineplax" cinemas.

Two other stadia are scheduled to be realized in the States in the near future: the more modest 20,000 seat Staples Center to be built in Los Angeles to the designs of Dan Meis and Derek McCullum[6] of the NBBJ/LA office and the 72,000 seat Paul Brown stadium to be built on the flood plain of the Cincinnati River, between the expressway and the water. This last, designed by Meis in collaboration with Paul Davis, does not include much by way of commercial space; however, the undercroft set to one side of the tribune will accommodate a number of luxurious club rooms, facing out over the city through a continuous curtain wall. Unlike the symmetrical San Nicola Stadium recently realized by the Italian architect Renzo Piano at Bari, or the Badalona basketball arena built to the designs of Catalan architects Bonell and

Rius, the central axis of this partially asymmetrical stadium lines up with a major autoroute entering into the city, thereby presenting the stadium as a symbol of the urban community. This "representational threshold" will be reinforced in this instance by a giant, double-sided, LED scoreboard, posting the state of play as much for the benefit of motorists as for the spectators in the stands. Like Henri Gaudin's asymmetrical stadium built at Charleroi outside Paris, the tribunes of this arena will be partially covered by cable-tied teflon canopies, suspended from steel bents cantilevering beyond the upper rim of the stadium. This superstructure emphasizes the partially divided character of the arena, which in its turn reinforces the spiralling topography of the artificial ground rising up either side above the attendant multi-storey parking. The "crescents" of the two halves of the stadium, with their all too literal allusion to American football shoulder pads distantly recall the reference that Maki made to samurai helmets in the shell roof of his Fujisawa Gymnasium (1985).

The ovoid plan of the typical stadium also seems to carry over uncannily into many of the recent high-rise proposals made by the Pran team for South East Asia where the developments are often predicated on a quasi-ovoid plan surrounded on all sides by a spread-eagled podium. This is patently so in the case of the 50-storey Graha Kuningan tower project under construction in Jakarta between 1995 and 1998.[7] Here, aside from three levels of underground parking, the podium contains a wide variety of services in order to provide a convenient self-contained twelve-hour environment for the personnel who work in the building. Thus we find the additional complement of a bank, a discotheque, a karaoke bar and a VIP sky lobby. This last, dedicated to an interexchange between express and local elevators, assures the building an efficiency factor of 87%, 2% higher than the norm for vertical access in high-rise structures. This was accomplished by the use of double-decker shuttle elevators, which distribute tenants from the ground level to a sky lobby on the 35th and 36th levels. Thus there are no more than two lift sets (four elevators per set) in either the low, mid or high sections at any one time. This technical arrangement gave Pran the necessary freedom to be able to manipulate the plan profile of the building envelope. Hence the space-age imagery of the tower, culminating in the prow-like pinnacle of the building, which is topped by a telecommunications mast.

In one high-rise proposal after another Pran returns to this aerodynamic paradigm; one that often serves to differentiate between two sides of a tower. We encounter something similar in the Karet Tower, also projected for downtown Jakarta in 1995, where the bent back of one side of the high-rise dematerialises as it curves over the roof of the structure in the form of a perforated canopy. This variation of the bent slab block also serves to warp the Portofino Tower projected for Miami, Florida, in 1994. A similar back-versus-front theme determines the high-rise image of the SBS tower projected for Seoul, Korea in 1995, along with the El Presidente slab designed for Manila in the Philippines in 1997. In this last instance the "back" is in fact the service core that serves to shield the building from the sun while the bulging "front" of the opposing curtain-wall turns its leading edge into the wind like a spinnaker.

Among Pran's proposals for South East Asia, none is of such consequence in urbanistic terms, as his Mangarai Transportation Centre projected in 1996.[8] Here twenty-two rail lines, plus four high-speed, bullet-train tracks feed into an arena-like station that is flanked on both sides by inter- and inner-city bus termini. The tracks are enclosed and overlaid by two successive layers of retail accommodation and by a mezzanine restaurant from which one may obtain a panoramic view of the tracks. Escalators, elevators and stairs link the different levels, while various side canopies and wide-span, shell roofs are carried over the terminus on swept-back steel supports mounted off the platforms. The transportation hub is in fact the centre of a master plan for the entire area although at this stage the character of the surrounding neighbourhood has been left somewhat vague.

What we may call the generic megaform approach has informed the most recent efforts of the Pran team in two other typical strategies. The first of these may be characterized as an urban vortex in which a dominating high-rise shaft is flanked by medium- to low-rise slabs that are designed so as to appear to gyrate around the central form. This is the case in the Kwun Tong Town Centre projected for Hong Kong in 1988,[9] where the central high-rise tops out at eighty-eight floors while the attendant buildings range from fourteen to sixty-five floors in height. The second approach is invariably applied to open, green-field sites. Typical of this was Pran's 1990 entry for a competition for the Rikshospital in Oslo. Invariably, Pran's green-field *parti* takes the form of a set of loosely-linked, finger-like, low-rise buildings. Irrespective of whether they are hospital wards, faculty buildings or offices, with each pavilion being connected to a continuous glazed gallery that in turn is fed by an automobile loop, interwoven with the landscape and with a network of pedestrian walkways. This paradigm, at different scales and with different detailed treatment, determines to all intents and purposes, both the project for Telenor in Oslo of 1998 and the design for the Reebok Headquarters in Boston,[10] this last being scheduled to start construction in the summer of 1998. Like the new Cincinnati Bengals Stadium, the elevated three-storey high gallery of the Reebok building has afforded an occasion for demonstrating the tectonic ability of the team for here the space has been enclosed by an ingenious, faceted window-wall. Engineered in collaboration with Advanced Structures Incorporated this wall has been broken into thirty-foot long panels supported by tied, cranked-steel trusses set at the same intervals. These panels are faceted in their turn by being further divided into ten-foot bays that are laterally stabilized by 2 1/2 inch diameter tubular steel cross-bracing. The glass wall, while totally stable, has a capacity to flex according to fluctuations in local wind pressure. It is clear that this Reebok "arcade" will serve as the model for the Telenor Plaza[11] in the Telenor Headquarters scheme for Norway which has recently been awarded to NBBJ as the result of a limited competition.

As the century comes to a close it is clear that sculptural form has entered the late modern architectural repertoire in a major way, although how this plasticity is generated and more importantly how this sculptural dimension is modulated and controlled varies from architect to architect. One needs to distinguish in this connection between plastic surfaces, which are generated and supported by manifest structural and spatial matrices, and surfaces that simply arise from the enclosure of rather arbitrarily contoured volumes. In the case of Piano's Osaka airport, Maki's Fujisawa Gymnasium, and Enric Miralles's Alicante Gymnastic Centre, it is evident that the shell-like surfaces which determine the outer form are inseparable from the structural/space systems over which they are laid. Moreover in each of these works the overall plastic effect, at both the macro and the micro level depends on the intermediate jointing systems and on the precise quality of the junctions that obtain between the undulating facets of the shell-form and the supporting structural network. It is just this dialect which is absent from Frank Gehry's rhetorical *tour de force* in Bilbao where the total suppression of the support structure (unavoidable perhaps given the inelegance), reduces the Guggenheim in Bilbao to a gigantic piece of sculpture which "narcissistically" competes with the sculptures and other art works that it happens to contain.

When it comes to the curtain-wall sheathing of contoured volumes, irrespective of whether the skin is made out of metal, stone, wood or glass, a question arises as to the generic nature of the enveloped space, one which cannot be entirely separated from the environmental conditions that necessarily derive from the interaction between the membrane and the climate. We need to note that the *a priori* continuity of the sculptural form of a building may readily come into conflict with its orientation as Kenny Yeang has demonstrated in a number of ecologically responsive high-rise buildings. It is obvious that such buildings may be as much subject to climate control as any other building type and that this could potentially be a source of ornamental form as it once was in the heyday of the Neo-Corbusian *brise soleil*. It is but a step from the *brise soleil* to the thermal wall as this has been recently refined by Renzo Piano in his Potsdamerplatz office building, a highly sophisticated approach which patently merits examination by the Pran team as do the organic attributes of Piano's aerodynamically profiled high-rise tower recently developed for Sydney, Australia. Clearly clients may be just as well served by such technological refinements as by the sculptural dynamism of a given gestalt and indeed these two factors may be readily brought to reinforce each other.

Evidently free form cannot be limited solely by such considerations but free form like free verse cannot, on the other hand, be solely determined by intuition. And while one cannot exclusively restrict this modus to mathematically warped surfaces or to cybernetic morphing of various kinds, organic form has nonetheless its own autonomy, empathetically deriving from nature and from deepseated feelings for the waxing and waning of natural forms and processes. This was surely latent in the work of Erich Mendelsohn, whose sense of rhythmic emergence and feeling for the plastic culmination of a movement was exemplary. Much serves to separate his laconic sharpness and sense of restraint from the rather mechanical application of streamlining that was to characterize a great deal of plastic form from the nineteen twenties to the early thirties. To intend a poetic of movement is to evoke many metaphorical issues at once since architecture, unlike machinery, does not move. At the same time the potential of plastic form to determine the topography of any work, not only of a building but also of the landscape which surrounds it and upon which it depends, has already been amply demonstrated by the Pran team on many different occasions. One only hopes that as they begin to realize their first works of consequence they will have an opportunity to assess where they stand particularly with regard to the entire legacy of the modern movement and with respect to the severe conditions that will inevitably confront the culture of architecture as it enters the next century.

As NBBJ prepares its ranks for the challenge of the future, the architecture of Peter Pran proffers itself as a continuing experiment, as an alternative mode of practice currently sponsored with generosity and foresight by one of the largest firms in the country.[12] It is difficult to characterize in any succinct way the unique role that Pran plays in this endeavour as he continually passes in and out of a shifting spectrum of responsibilities; part visionary, part ideas man, part designer, part roving critic, part negotiator, part policy-maker and, above all, an architect for a new age, where neither the individual practice nor the corporate firm will remain the same and where the hybrid alternative will begin to have a greater chance of achieving work of quality.

Opening at the New York State Psychiatric Institute

1 From Jonathan Ward's article "Topographic Movement" in this book.

2 Designed by Pran in collaboration with Timothy Johnson and Jill Lerner.

3 This design gained first prize in a limited competition that included Norman Foster, Rafael Viñoly, Robert Venturi, and Edward Larrabie Barnes. Pran's collaborators on this occasion included Timothy Johnson and Paul Davis.

4 Designed by Timothy Johnson and Jonathan Ward.

5 Designed in collaboration with Jonathan Ward and Joey Myers.

6 Dan Meis was also the designer of the Saitama Stadium, Tokyo, Japan, now under construction. This work was acquired through a limited competition against Richard Rogers, Jean Nouvel, and Rem Koolhaas.

7 Designed by Pran together with Paul Davis, Timothy Johnson, and Jonathan Ward.

8 Designed by Pran, Jonathan Ward, Jin Ah Park, and Dorman Anderson.

9 Designed by Pran, Jonathan Ward, Joey Myers, Dorman Anderson, and Jim Jonassen.

10 The leading designer in this case was Jonathan Ward together with the principal Steve McConnell of NBBJ and senior designer Jin Ah Park.

11 Telenor is designed by Pran, Joey Myers, Jonathan Ward, Scott Wyatt, Jin Ah Park, and Curtis Wagner.

12 It should be noted that NBBJ is the second largest firm in the United States and the fifth largest internationally.

Peter Pran and the Modern Position
Juhani Pallasmaa

Peter Pran is a fervent believer in modernism. The fierce post-modernist polemic of the early 1980s and the concurrent attacks on the established traditions of modernism only helped to reinforce and re-define his modernist stance. The title of one of Pran's essays, "A Complete Commitment to a Continued and New Modern Architecture,"[1] expresses his credo and architectural manifesto. The failure of the post-modern ideology to produce architecture evoking a sense of authentic culture has given a new significance to the modernist position. Partly as a conscious reaction to the critique, the modernist attitude has produced an unforeseen array of architectural explorations.

Peter Pran has a long and varied professional background and today he is one of the most devoted and productive members of the new modernist front. Most architects tend to become softer and more permissive as they age, but Peter Pran's radical attitude seems to toughen with time. In his inspired work today, he combines the architectural passion of his mentor Mies van der Rohe, a desire for architectural innovation through the exploitation of the newest construction materials, techniques and computerized design methods, and the Nordic sobriety of his birthplace, Norway. Regardless of his radical architectural imagery, Pran has been exceptionally successful in architectural competitions, and this speaks of his rigorous functional and technical realism. Pran's projects range from business headquarters and office towers to academic buildings, from hospitals and research centres to psychiatric institutes, and from airport terminal structures to gigantic stadia and convention or entertainment centres. Although he has lived and worked in the United States since 1963, Pran still carries the Nordic modernist set of mind, which is reflected in the morality and logic of his work as it expands to an ever wider geographic ground. His projects already cover the globe: the USA, Canada, England, Japan, the Netherlands, Norway, Ecuador, Saudi Arabia, Indonesia.

Since the architectural profession in America tends to either associate with the economic establishment or produce theoretical, programmatic projects outside societal reality, it is illuminating to view the Nordic architectural position inherited by Pran.

In the Nordic countries the Functionalist morality, and modernity in general, have traditionally been interwoven with the development of Nordic democracy and the ideal of the Welfare State. Instead of being a position of aesthetic opposition, modernity has served as an ideological confirmation, aspiring to materialize ideals of progress and democracy from within the societal reality. Modern architecture, design and aesthetic culture have been regarded as constituents of the societal reality itself. The Nordic view of culture, art and aesthetics reflects a strong ethical ingredient. Design is not considered as a matter of individualistic expression but as a societal responsibility, weaving together political, cultural and economic as well as aesthetic aspirations. As a consequence, an element of idealization, a search for a societal ideal, is engraved in the notion of modernism. The idea of questioning the validity of modernity, not to speak of its outright rejection, seems irrelevant — if not totally absurd — in the Nordic context. Questioning the modernist position would imply the questioning of cultural evolution all together; to the Nordic modernist such a thought would appear as the absurd attitude of an architect who has never been granted a real role in the construction of his society.

The architectural development of the past fifteen years has made it clear that in its essence modernism is not a visual stylistic canon at all but a dialectic philosophical position in relation to the reality of culture. The modernist position is an attitude of repeated re-readings of the past as well as of the present human condition. It is a continuous process of questioning the accepted cultural convention. The modernist places himself in a dialogue between the past and the present, collective and individual, convention and innovation. In this dialectic tension neither opposite is given an *a priori* supremacy; the unique balance between the opposites is sought in each individual case.

While acknowledging tradition, the modernist questions it, and consequently keeps redefining the cornerstones of existential reality and of the artistic tradition. This dialectical process constantly re-evaluates the understanding of history; continuous re-reading and judgement keeps revealing artistic works that have previously been bypassed in the accepted view of history and discards works that have occasionally been given undue merit.

"The *Quixote* that we read is not that of Cervantes, any more than our *Madame Bovary* is that of Flaubert. Each twentieth-century reader involuntarily rewrites in his own way the masterpieces of past centuries,"[2] writes André Maurois in his preface to Jorge Luis Borges' *Labyrinths*. No doubt, the spaces and situations of every literary masterpiece are recreated by the reader at each reading. The labyrinthine complexities of *The Library of Babel* are imaginings of the reader. Nor is the history of architecture a petrified and given past. Every architect who seeks an authentic experiential basis in his work is bound to redefine and redesign the masterpieces of history through his own creative endeavour.

T.S. Eliot gives an illuminating view of the complexities of time and artistic tradition: "Tradition is a matter of much wider significance. It cannot be inherited, and if you want it you must obtain it by great labour. It involves, in the first place, the historical sense. ... And the historical sense involves a perception, not only of the pastness of the past, but of its presence; the historical sense compels a man to write not merely with his own generation in his bones, but with a feeling that the whole of the literature ... has a simultaneous existence and composes a simultaneous order."[3]

The modernist position is aware of the inherent tension between societal convention and the aspirations of the creative individual. The modernist realizes that the present is not a fatalistic consequence of the past, but a product of desires, deliberate choices and decisions. An architect participates consciously in the making of the future, and without the image of an ideal the making of architecture becomes absurd. The decades since the emergence of modernity have, however, revealed the naiveté of the modernist societal mission of architecture, as proclaimed by Le Corbusier in *Towards a New Architecture*. The course of cultural evolution seems to be fundamentally beyond the means of design and of deliberate control. Nevertheless, the currently diminishing role of architecture in societal values represents a renewed mission for architecture in providing a metaphysical frame for human existence.

Peter Pran exemplifies the current redefinition of the modernist *ethos*, as well as the quest to expand the territory of the art of architecture. The essence of Pran's recent work is the de-construction of the closed and unambiguously delineated architectural volume. He aspires to emancipate this architectural volume from its gravity, opacity and mass, and to turn architecture into an interacting field of dematerialized and weightless movement. Whereas early modernist buildings aspired to a weightless horizontal flow, Peter Pran conceives curved and warped movements that fuse horizontality with verticality, and rectangularity with curved geometries.

The dominant spaces of Pran are interstitial ravine-like gaps in the interacting field of different geometries. The great spaces of classical architecture and early modernism are centres around which the architectural ensemble organizes itself, whereas the dramatic spaces of Pran are in-between spaces, spatial events that appear as accidental and arbitrary occurrences in the juxtaposition of conflicting geometries. This seems to express a deliberate avoidance of a static architectural focus or strong *gestalt*. Peter Pran's architecture is a curvilinear development of De Stijl's planar compositions, of the dynamic Suprematist configurations of Malevich and the Constructivist virtual volumes of El Lissitsky hovering weightlessly in the air. Pran's inspiration drawn from modern sculpture is equally evident. His recent projects bring to mind the early constructivist sculptures of Naum Gabo and Antoine Pevsner. The virtual movement of Constantin Brancusi's sculpture is also apparent in the animistic imagery concealed in Pran's projects like the *Mixed-use Tower* and the *Graha Kuningan* and *Karet Office Towers* in Jakarta.

In Pran's recent designs, surfaces are losing their uniformity; walls are going through a process of peeling off that reveals hidden layers and veins behind the immediate architectural skin. The contradictory aspirations for gravity and flight, *stasis* and movement, mass and void, are inherent in the very phenomenon of architecture. In Peter Pran's new-modernist architecture the gravity and calm *stasis* of Mies turns into sensations of suspension, flight, collision and accelerated speed.

On the threshold of the third millennium architecture is searching for new directions on two opposite fronts: the re-identification of the mytho-poetic basis of architecture, and the expansion of architectural expression into the new terrain of complexity, uncertainty and velocity. Pran's work is placed on the latter frontier.

The current interest in the expressive possibilities of the curved wall or warped volume among architects ranging from Alvaro Siza and Tadao Ando to the de-constructivists invites a psychoanalytical interpretation. Is the curve a metaphor for the liberation of architecture from the domination of the urban grid, repetitiousness and the right angle? Does it signal an emergence of a female sensuality and eroticism in the traditionally masculine world of construction? Does the fascination with the curve suggest a new tactility? Is the avoidance of finitely enclosed space an expression of a desire to defy the power of the centre?

The current fascination with curved geometries also reflects the liberating impact of the computer, which facilitates conception and numerical definition of complex curvilinear juxtapositions, intersections and interpenetrations. The moulded architectural spaces of the craft age, from the masterpieces of Bavarian Rococo to Alvar Aalto, did not demand precise dimensional pre-definition, whereas today's processes of prefabrication require exact mathematical modelling, and this can only be achieved by means of the computer. Peter Pran's architectural concepts may not be generated initially by the computer, but their presentation and numerical description are facilitated, if not actually made possible, by the computer.

The distinct ambience of architectural styling in Pran's work and his use of linear surface motifs, conceived to accelerate a sense of movement, re-create an air redolent of Art Deco. In view of the historical fact that the vigorous Art Deco Movement in America of the 1920s and 1930s was interrupted by the more seriously tectonic architecture of the immigrant generation of European modernists, Pran's neo-modern architecture interestingly reconnects with this indigenous line of American modernity.

Apart from the architectural quality of Pran's projects, the fact that these daringly experimental schemes have been produced within some of the largest architectural practices in America is significant. Undeniably, works of high architectural quality, even masterpieces, have been conceived by large corporate firms in America. As a rule, however, corporate design tends to utilize conventional imageries and technologies, and the materialized work rarely conveys the presence of the magic touch of a creative hand. It is evident that a large design team tends to emphasize intellectual and rational characteristics of concept and imagery over spontaneous, irrational and subconscious dimensions, those which can be sustained only by a creative individual. The absence of the creative individual is accentuated by the domination of visual imagery at the cost of the tactile realm. Large scale corporate construction also tends to lack tectonic reality and material presence as a consequence of the aspiration for a striking image, and the use of construction methods devoid of human labour and the humanising touch of the craftsman.

The creative work of Pran and his associates and assistants suggests a possibility of breaking down corporate design organizations into smaller studio teams to provide a different set of creative mental and psychological prerequisites. In Pran's case, the corporate base seems to serve as a fertile financial and professional support in the production of convincing avant-garde work.

The realities of construction and use constitute the essential test for the validity of architectural ideas. Regrettably, most of Pran's energetic architectural projects of the last decade have not been executed but they constitute an impressive series of studies in the possibilities of an architectural language. The material presence and spatial authority of his new modern architecture can be experienced in the executed examples of the *Deloitte & Touche Headquarters Executive Area* in Wilton, Connecticut, the *New York State Psychiatric Institute* in Manhattan, and the *Academic Buildings of the Binghamton University* in New York State. We sincerely hope that Peter Pran will be able to execute more of his recent projects, and thus put his passionate ideas through the ultimate reality test of architecture. His long and exceptionally varied professional experience and unwavering passion for architectural quality are a sure guarantee of the achievement of this result.

1 Peter Pran, "A Complete Commitment to a continued and new Modern Architecture,' *Peter Pran of Ellerbe Becket: Recent Works*, Architectural Monographs No. 24, Academy Editions, London, 1992, pp. 8-9.

2 André Maurois, "Preface" to Jorge Luis Borges, *Labyrinths*, Penguin Books, London, 1970, p. 12.

3 T.S. Eliot, "Tradition and the Individual Talent" (1919) in *Selected Essays*, new edition, Harcourt, Brace & World, New York, 1964.

A Personal Statement
Daniel Libeskind

It is not often that I am asked to provide an introduction to a book which deals with an architect whose work is part of the corporate world. I have followed with interest, however, the architectural work of Peter Pran, since he surely represents the best in the large American architectural firms.

His personal commitment to architecture has been to elevate, through his energy and his own considerable creative talent, the often banal and expedient to the level of large-scale innovation and the untested.

The contents of this book offer an impressive array of commercial works which attempt to expand the limits of corporate architecture and establish a new and potentially exciting realm.

An Architecture of Movement in Time and Space: Altered Perceptions
Peter Pran, Jonathan Ward, Jin Ah Park, Joey Myers

An architecture of altered perceptions aims at two slightly paradoxical goals: to build places that inspire and shelter; to simultaneously skew the perspective of the inhabitant and offer a perception of life and art and our place in the world which is perhaps unknown or unthought of.

The building designs are site specific, and innovative concepts are expressed in a poetry of movement and fluency, from which the resulting freedom manifests itself in the liberating work. It is also an expression of current cultural/social movements and the movement of time while renewing our perception of daily life. The forms and folds of both natural and urban topography inform the building to dance in a certain way. The building must be able to dance as a lone dancer and in a chorus line and not lose its potency. The building should know when and where it is appropriate to be grounded, bowing to the forces of gravity, and when it must break free and express the constant desire of humans to defy nature and push optimistically into the future.

There needs to be a dialectic relationship between the aesthetic/poetic/conceptual and the inner reality. It is crucial to transform the conceptual ideas and images about the site and the function of the place into an understanding of structure/material/construction which moves towards a very real tectonic realization of the architecture. Contemporary architecture becomes relevant when it defines the spirit of a place and creates new unseen realities through an insistent and bold exploration. Our architecture tries to move the inhabitant of the city and the building itself to question our path in life and to live and communicate in better ways. There is a fluid liberating spirit in the work which attempts to understand the past and learn from it while defying it and allowing the place to express its social and cultural freedom.

Computer animation brings movement and time, which are its major components, to the experience of architecture, and makes architecture more understandable. The computer meets the requirement for fast production, while extending the designer's opportunity for exploring on the cutting edge of progress many other built realities, a new world of three-dimensional plasticity, richness and complexity. The electronic world expressed through architecture is the future.

Shifting and altered perceptions allow the inhabitants to open up new doors in their thinking, which shed new light on old ways of life and interaction. Courageous architecture is achieved through a visionary spirit that reflects the inner changing forces of our society. Authentic architecture creates cultural statements of our times.

The tools that allow us to struggle with the medium of architecture must be varied in order to tap into avenues of thought and inspiration which will be closed if architects limit themselves to a singular way of investigation. The computer has allowed us to open up a new world of three-dimensional plasticity, richness, and complexity, which only the mind's eye could fathom only a few years ago. We can now explore the forms, spaces, and connections in a facile real-time mode in which we can make better and faster decisions.

The computer also allows us to add materiality, light, and the critical fourth dimension, time, to the design process. These understandings that are so fundamental to architecture, but are often abstracted to the level of absurdity in the traditional design process, must be captured in this architecture. We are also using the computer to help us to construct the things which ten years ago existed only in our imagination. This, in the end, becomes just another tool in the process of unfolding these altered perceptions.

The building designs are dedicated to the life and history of the city or place we work in. Quality modern architecture developed in countries all over the globe creates a shared culture through a common, universally understood and appreciated design language.

The contemporary materials of glass and metal communicate a transparency in architecture that permits a multiple layered reading, quite different from the solid masonry of earlier centuries. Contemporary architects bring these options and expressions into their work.

The nostalgic tendency to freeze cities to their old building images from the 1960s, 1930s or earlier periods (the shallow waters of traditional "contextualism" which America is particularly enamoured with), and not to allow innovative modern architecture is deadly. It does not merely ensure that those cities stand still; they regress.

The twenty-year old regressive postmodern historicist movement has clearly fizzled out in recent years, but unfortunately it has turned into a quietly accepted traditional-oriented soft postmodern style, where the main goal is to "fit in" with older settings by repeating them; about half of all building design jobs in America go to firms that can produce such work — often at the insistence of developers and public officials. This failure of nerve has spread through North America denying opportunities for authentic modern architects. Copied traditionalism represents an undermining of the struggle of earlier modernists and of the work of today's rigorous modern architects.

Buildings require an ethical and socio-political commitment to the public realm; the design of buildings of content, integrity and inquiry transforms our cultural and political life progressively. Authentic architecture becomes a work of art.

A building without an idea is a dead building. Architecture is meaningful when it is brought to the level of thought and poetry.

Topographic Movement
Jonathan Ward

The collaborative group of architects led by Peter Pran with Tim Johnson, Paul Davis, and Jonathan Ward, has been striving to create an architecture of topographic movement. The term topo-graphic moves beyond the limits of hills and woods to encompass our whole approach. The goal is to describe the movement of place (as suggested by the connotations of the word topo-graphic). We try to avoid endless rationalizations and banal rules and regulations and try instead to capture the movements of our time and the spirit of the place (both physical and psychological), the place created within, and the people who dwell in that place. The architecture is approached through both intuitive and objective layers of thought. This mode allows the folds, structures, and movements of the site, the inhabitants, programme, needs, light, and society at large to suggest and indeed mould the architecture. This is achieved, more often than not, through an experiential, improvisational mode, not unlike John Coltrane expressing his feelings and interacting with those around him through his music. The beauty of the creation of a place to dwell in is the act of resolving the topographic forces that weave through the site and around the need and desire for this place to exist.

The forces that drive an architecture of topographic movement govern the way we work, the individuals who create the work, the design tools and methods, and the desire to create an architecture that alters perceptions of the mundane movements of life.

The way in which any work of art is created or any public endeavour undertaken is clearly tied to the way it is made — the process. The work that is represented here is the work of a collaborative — not a collective — and certainly not the usual architectural dictatorship. It is an attempt to move away from the typical modes of the corporate firm and the small iconoclast firm and define a different way of working that results in a unique product. The collaborative is by definition ephemeral and ever-changing depending on the desires of the individuals involved at any given time. The collective is the worst situation in which to practise architecture. In a collective it is assumed that all players are equal and everyone has an equal say. This leads to an extreme watering down of the ideas that stimulate power, clarity and beauty in architecture. It is a mode that is often practised in larger firms. We have attempted to create an anomaly within the large firm where we primarily practise by advocating the elimination of the collective, which is responsible for so much of the mediocre work surrounding us today: the ambivalent, the ambiguous, the unsure, the saccharine, the empty pastiche of a democratic, bureaucratic thought process. With the resources of a large firm, held together by a pool of diverse skills and talents, with both financial and physical resources, the possibilities are great. The bottom line is that everyone has different strengths and weaknesses which should be balanced; we are, after all, individuals.

In contrast to the collective is the dictatorship. The leadership of the design vision and the direction of the practice must be clear and focused; otherwise the architecture and the livelihood of the firm are compromised. The dictatorship can lead to superb work, but in the end the environment is so stifling that any errant creativity is stamped out and ideas become stale. In a dictatorship talent flows through the office like a broken water main, filtering ideas, spewing out empty architects. For ideas to grow and progress they must be constantly fed in a healthy manner. Relationships, ideas, and directions must grow.

The collaborative is the mode in which we operate. This way of working and interacting finds its parallel in jazz. In a jazz ensemble there is a powerful balance between the vision and sound of the group and the spark, creativity and voice of the individual musician. The group is only as good as its worst member. This is a reality of life where individual human beings all have different abilities, sensitivities and outlooks on life itself. Within the jazz ensemble each individual player has a task which makes the whole move and sing. The drummer will lay down the beat and ensure that the groove is always in forward momentum. The bass holds down the bottom as well as solidifying the time, playing counterpoint to the upper harmonies and melodies and the rhythms of the drums. The piano meshes the harmonies, the rhythms, and the melody simultaneously. The horns then sing and weave above the dancing structure. Some or all the members arrange tunes or contribute original material. On top of these obligations each voice has ample opportunity to sing and express its individual soul, the mood of the day, and reflect the vibe of the place. The players must also have the ability to play with others of equal or higher ability and expression.

We are all educated in the language and nuances of the architectural profession, and we can work as a group effectively because of common goals, understandings, and desires to always progress and find a new layer to the topographic movement. But what really makes the work exciting and stimulating is the fact that we each have a strong voice. Despite our individuality and diverse backgrounds we have the ability to compose and arrange, formulate and develop architecture with a simultaneity that parallels that of the jazz ensemble. Each designer is interested in different aspects. We promote the synthesis by breaking the projects into parts; each designer pushes and pulls one area and then the group works to resolve the melodies of the individual parts. This way of working lends itself to weaving egos and expressions into topographic movements.

The group is somewhat ephemeral at times, yet always connected by the common goal of creating an architecture that responds to and alters the movement of the world around us at any given time. Peter Pran has acted as the lightning rod, believing in the collaborative rather than the dictatorship, and has become the rallying point for a group of young, energetic designers. The seeds were planted in the New York and Minneapolis offices of Ellerbe Becket in the late 1980s. In 1986 Peter was hired by Wayne Fishback, the former director of the New York Ellerbe Becket office, and John Gaunt, former CEO of Ellerbe Becket, as a design principal in the New York office. This was an era in which Ellerbe, under the helm of the visionary leadership of Gaunt, was determined to prove that corporate architecture could and should be forward thinking, beautiful, ground breaking, and powerful. Gaunt set the tone by shunning the banal collectivism that many call corporate architecture. Peter led the visual charge, allied with other visionaries in the firm such as Merdad Yazdani in the LA office, Mick Johnson in the Minneapolis office, Carlos Zapata in the New York Office, and Mark Molen in the Washington office. Timothy Johnson, Paul Quinn and Jonathan Ward all came from the Minneapolis office and were drawn by the energy that Peter and Carlos, along with Eduardo Calma, Curtis Wagner, Maria Wilthew and Lyn Rice were creating out East.

Initially it was the competitions in which we were involved with Peter (based on his vast experience and his will to push our ideas to the forefront of the architecture community and onto the international stage), that were the microcosms for the fermentation and growth of our intellectual and design development. Tim Johnson eventually moved to New York to pursue the development of this own body of thought and work with Peter and Carlos Zapata. Paul Davis continued to go back and forth, playing a leading role in the design of the winning scheme for the New York Police Academy. I went on to work with Mark Molen at the Washington DC office of Ellerbe Becket but was eventually drawn to New York, first for a series of competitions and then a complete move and full immersion in the work.

The first time any of us worked with Peter was always a trial, much like the cutting sessions of the jazz world when the new player comes into the club and challenges the band to let him sit in and try to cut them... pushing the force of new melodic, harmonic, or rhythmic ideas and energy into the music and gaining a spiritual and creative bond with the musicians. The new ideas in our case are usually formal expression, tectonic desires and functional idiosyncrasies, but the same bond and creative development ensue in our work. The first time that I found myself in New York for a two week competition for a new psychiatric hospital in Miami, Florida, it was indeed a cutting session. Peter had never met me, and had no idea what my skills were. Eyeing me sceptically, he asked me to explore some ideas for the project in a physical model. We talked briefly about some of the force lines on the site and some of the emotional movements he felt about the project type and the city around it. We also went through the programme, client goals and some basic functional diagrams. I cut out a few schemes that passed muster and revealed a bond that linked to our pursuit of an architecture of topographic movement for the next six years.

Many of the forces behind the earlier work were revealed to me while I was working in Minneapolis in the early 1990s, well before I moved to Washington or New York. My path immediately collided with that of Paul Davis. Paul is at once outrageous, driven, and an incredibly kind mentor. I worked with him, observing his work and ideas. Many of the forces and folded perceptions of the early work were driven by Paul. His outlook on life was inspiring in that it was a journey towards a fresh take on life and

work, while at the same time challenging the complacent mores of our office environment and society at large with a half submerged seriousness that is both clear and focused. An incredible counter culture spun around Paul at Ellerbe Becket. Minneapolis was the corporate headquarters where Gaunt promoted a freedom that was to open up the possibilities of a corporate architecture firm to create works that would inspire those who would live in them. The Ghetto, as it was called, was created in the bowls of the medical division but soon erupted in other areas of the office, and in other offices and other firms. The environment was charged with imagery, found objects, music, dim lights and a free exchange of ideas and banter about life and work. Much of this energy was drawn from the unique individuals in Minneapolis, much imported from New York. The Ghetto was augmented by a group of designers in the middle of corn fields (a formula of obviously limited shelf life): Jeff Walden, Dave Koenen, Derek McCallum, Michael Kennedy, and Tim Carl. This energy and collaborative spirit has kept us all going despite our subsequent diaspora.

Tim Johnson, who left the Ghetto and moved to New York to work with Peter and Carlos, soon found himself stepping into Carlos's role when he left Ellerbe to form his own firm in Miami. Tim was instrumental in driving the work into built reality. Competitions are still an active part of the creation of the architectural ideas — always challenging the norm and never falling into the rut of sameness. But the real challenge is to build the ideas and make them part of our physical environment enabling those who dwell in them to see the world differently. The New York Psychiatric Institute was started by Peter and Curtis, and developed by Peter and Tim in collaboration with Dave Rova, Jim Chin, Jill Lerner, Mark Molen, Laura Ettelman, Maria Wilthew and others. This project on the Hudson River under the gaze of the George Washington Bridge was a tectonic testing ground for our ideas on topographic movement.

When I came to New York I was keenly interested in developing the reality of the work while maintaining the energy of the ideas. I worked with Tim to create a clear direction. A key development was our emergence in the Asian market. This acted as a catalyst to cement the two directions that any visionary architecture must follow: the balance between ideas that are experimental and provoke that altered perception we are striving for, and the tectonic reality of the architecture. The cities in Asia before the crash (symbolic though this may be) were seeking a visionary urban environment to complement their visionary economic and social development, which will continue despite economic setbacks. Many have no history of a city or an architecture symbolizing freedom, a free market economy, and a clear thrust towards a better future. We studied larger and larger mixed use and urban design projects, opening up our perspective on the impact of our work on the modern urban fabric.

Tim and I also collaborated on a critical project for the New York Transit Authority, now under construction. It honed our abilities to infuse our ideas into a restrictive group of users backed by a complex web of bureaucracy and politics, with serious budgetary constraints. The finished building will be tight but with a distinct movement and force rooted in our process and ideas.

The year 1996 saw a dramatic change when the corporate leaders of Ellerbe Becket decided to close the New York office, reduce their resources and practise architecture more conservatively, leading to the departure of most of the leading designers.

Peter and I chose to join NBBJ in Seattle, a large corporate firm with a strong desire to develop design directions and allow a multitude of possibilities while exploring the edge of architecture. Dorman Anderson, a friend of Peter's from their days working with Mies and a principal at NBBJ, made it happen and has proved a wonderful collaborator on several key projects. The support of the partners, in particular Jim Jonassen, David Hodemaker, Bill Bain, John Pangrazzio and Scott Wyatt has inspired us in our new firm. Simultaneously, Paul Davis joined NBBJ in Los Angeles, a studio focusing on sports and entertainment projects. The office is headed by three Ellerbe expatriates — Mike Hallmark, Dan Meis and Ron Turner — who ran the Kansas City sports studio for Ellerbe and the Ellerbe LA office. Tim Johnson has gone on to pursue business opportunities in Indonesia and New York and to set up on his own. I continue to work with him.

At NBBJ we have gone forward into the built reality. We have pursued many design opportunities, some successful, some not, while helping, along with other talented architects at NBBJ, to inject a sense of topographic movement into the work.

This phase has brought two new players: Jin Ah Park and Joey Myers. We have also been joined by Curtis Wagner, formerly of the Ellerbe New York office. Joey is another product of the Minneapolis Ghetto. Jin Ah and Joey have been key to some of the current digital tools in the design process at NBBJ, as well as contributing a new direction to the work. We have worked with many different studios, offices and teams within NBBJ to progress further or to inspire a different view of architecture within NBBJ.

The process is a way of working within an ephemeral design studio. The tools that fuel the process have been critical to much of the conceptualization and some of the formal underpinning of the work. The computer, in its role of advancing spatial and formal ideas and developing a fluid medium around which several designers can work and collaborate simultaneously, has been the tool with the most noticeable impact, enabling us to use our imagination in a new, fresh manner. The concepts of movement, folded space, altered perceptions, fractured light, and virtual gravity assumptions were created in our imaginations while the computer elicited fresh perspectives and altered our perceptions of space and our relation to the sky and earth.

But the computer, while important in the development of the architecture and the way we work, remains an additional tool. We have always relied on physical models, from foam massing studies to more exact studies in plexiglas, wood and metal. Drawing and collage are also critical mediums. The computer provides an additional, completely opposite angle and frame of reference but was never an end product. We run it alongside physical models and drawings from the first concept so that it can properly influence the thought process and provide a layer of conflicting and supportive development concepts and realities.

The computer was championed by Peter in New York and Mick Johnson in the Minneapolis offices of Ellerbe Becket. They saw the enormous potential of visualizing architecture still in the imagination, both to present ideas and to advance them into a built reality. Largely because of Peter's

mentoring nature, it became a vehicle for many young designers to put their ideas forward. The question is always what can we use to advance our ideas and our architecture. The computer has evolved from stiff wire views, which we hand coloured and shadowed, to full force virtual simulations of the spaces as they will be, always adding a new twist to the work and the way we work.

Our ideas and the ephemeral collaborative are evolving but there is an underlying spirit that informs the work. The notion of topographic movement is encompassed in a simultaneous folding of expression of the contemporary dwelling, of what that dwelling might be and a desire to enable those who live in it to perceive the world through altered perceptions.

When observing the state of the built environment today, particularly in America where we practise, there is a great sense of emptiness, of ordinary and shoddy construction. It has become void of any deeper meaning and values. No ritual or emotion is expressed in the architecture. Today, most of America has lost the nerve to build and develop cities for a lasting tomorrow and a beautiful and uplifting today. The architecture of our cities, from the great monumental and civic places to the homes we live in, has become a vast sea of emptiness. Solidity has given way to the paper thin. Lasting records of a generation's dreams and customs have given way to a perpetual Dodge City with a temporary stagefront that refuses to assume the trappings of a permanent place of dwelling and interaction. Ordinary has become the rule of the day. But there must be a way to live and move within our cities which is of today and rooted in a movement forward. The topos must describe this forward momentum.

The architecture that we have been developing over the past decade is constantly trying to perceive the ordinary in a new light. It is, after all, human nature to seek the new in the course of understanding ourselves better and our place in an evolving planet. We believe that architecture should express the moment by understanding and learning from the past but never creating empty replications of it. The forms and spaces of our buildings are created by a modern expressionism constantly driving towards altered perceptions. The Expressionism of the early twentieth century gave way to a dry, dogmatic "modernism" where functionalist rule dominated. This was replaced by the knee jerk reaction of "post-modernism," an even emptier way of creating our built environment than the harsh functionalism of modernism. Today there is freedom from dogma and a better understanding of our past and present. But the movement towards an architecture of power, dreams, function, and expression is not widespread.

We are striving to find a way to capture that movement and to allow others to inhabit that spatial perception. We are challenging the world and especially contemporary American society to move beyond entrenched notions of what a building should be and to move towards what a building could be. Architecture should frame a vision of ourselves, of what we have been and what we could become.

One of five finalists in the international architectural competition, this is the design for the new $600 million American Airlines/Northwest Airlines Terminal Building at JFK Airport in New York, the first new terminal to be built at JFK for 30 years. It is one of only two finalists that received votes of support from the clients: AA/NW and Port Authority of New York and New Jersey.

The new AA/NA Terminal will, when fully developed, provide 44 aircraft gates. Approximately 13 gates will handle 747 aircraft; 80 percent of the traffic will be international flights and 20 percent domestic flights. International flights require Federal Inspection Services (FIS). To provide the maximum number of gates, one part of the new terminal will be a satellite that accommodates 44 gates, and also two 747 taxi-ways between the main terminal and the satellite. This innovative planning layout, with all support services and amenities, provides customers with the best possible, hassle-free experience that will soon attract new passengers in its own right.

The overall design has as its main statement and strength a long, curved, floating steel roof that seems to come out of the ground with no beginning and no end — the "endless roof." It spans the entire arrival and departure area. This elegantly and delicately detailed structure poetically expresses movement and flight. The design creates a feeling of anticipation and delight in passengers and celebrates many aspects of flying before take-off.

The glass cylinder adjacent to the floating steel roof contains the arrival/departure station for the automatic trains/vehicles going to and from the Transportation Centre, as well as the arrival/departure station for the automatic trains moving back and forth between the main terminal and the satellite. It also houses a special bar and restaurant cantilevered out into the large, round interior atrium with a panoramic view of all the airplanes arriving and departing.

Consolidated Terminal for American Airlines/Northwest Airlines John F. Kennedy International Airport New York, USA, 1989

The arrival and departure floors are located in the main terminal, which is covered and enclosed by the large floating steel floor. The departure level has ticketing and concession stands, with restaurants and bars on the mezzanine level above.

The existing terminals at JFK Airport, with one exception, are representative of the more static modern architecture of the 1950s-1960s, the exception being Eero Saarinen's TWA terminal, with its beautiful central interior space. A large number of airport terminals around the world today look like suburban office buildings. This new AA/NA Terminal fits in with and embraces the existing airport bringing out its full architectural potential.

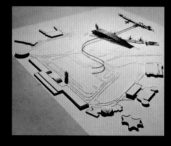

Client: American Airlines/Northwest Airlines
Port Authority of New York and New Jersey
Architects: Leibowitz/Ellerbe Becket:
Ellerbe Becket, New York: Peter Pran, Senior Vice President, Design Principal-in-Charge
Carlos Zapata, Design Director and Vice President
B. Wayne Fishback, Senior Vice President; Administrative Principal
Curtis Wagner, Project Designer
Eduardo Calma, Project Designer
Frank Yu, Designer
Maria Wilthew, Designer
Darius Sollohub, Designer
Vatche Aslanian, Designer
The Office of David Elliot Leibowitz:
David Leibowitz, President, Principal-in-Charge
Gilbert E. Balog, Senior Vice President, Principal-in-Charge of Programming and Planning
James Robinson, Planner
Mohammed Reza Samil, Planner
Albert Henning, Planner
Antonio Rodriguez, Planner
Keith Doble, Planner
Photographer: Dan Cornish

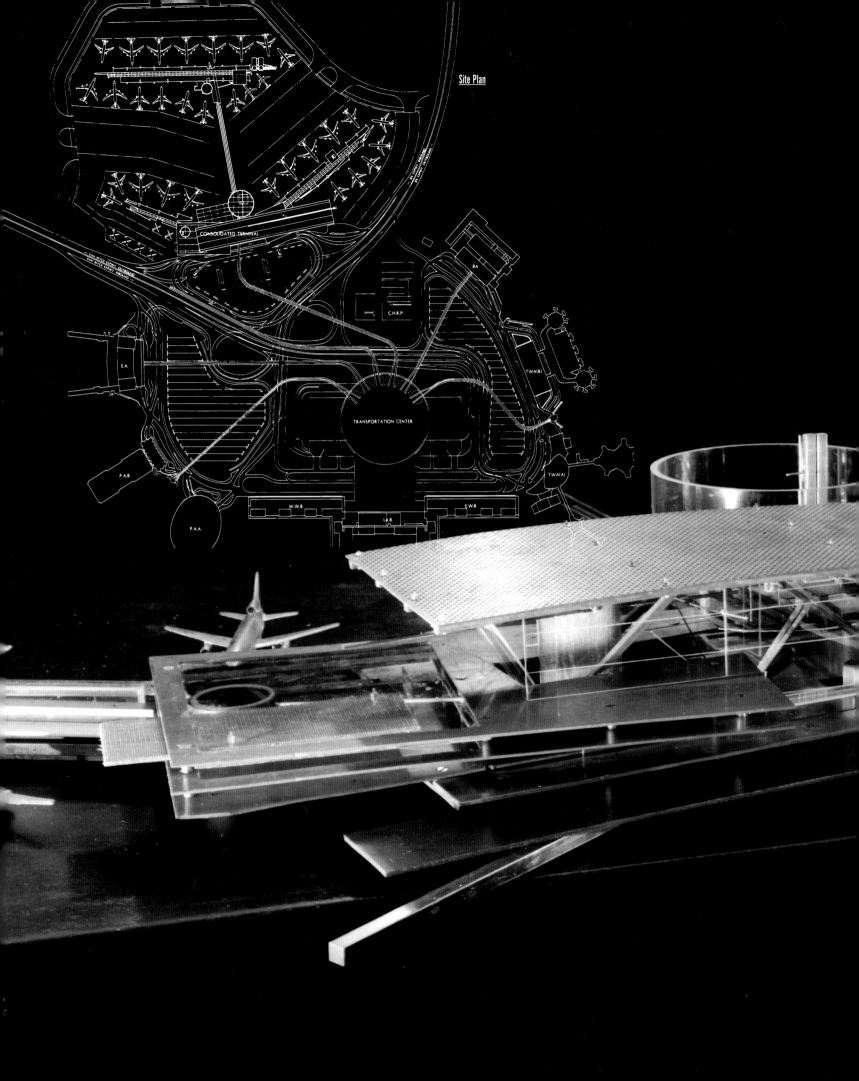

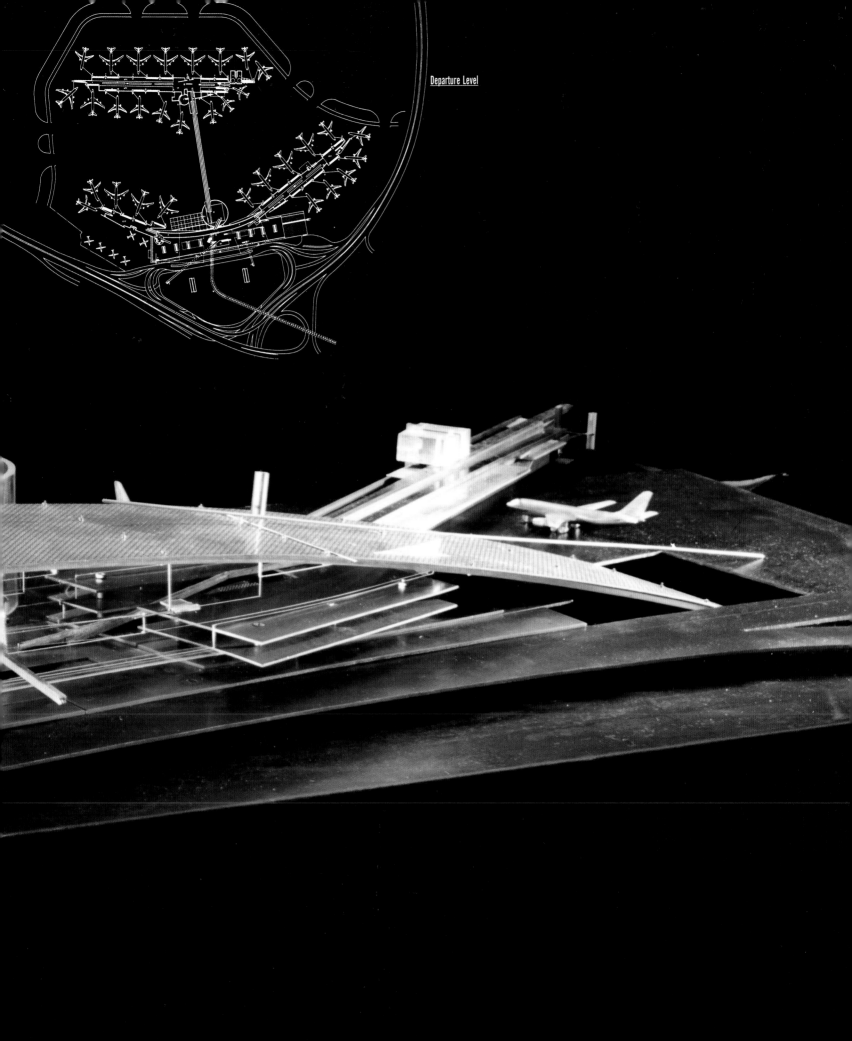

Departure Level

The design for this building, which won first prize in an international/national architecture competition, is for the new headquarters for *Aftenposten* and *Verdens Gang*, the two largest newspapers in Norway. The building site is located along Akersgaten, the main newspaper street in Oslo, adjacent to the two existing newspaper buildings. It is opposite three main Government Buildings and two blocks away from the Parliament Building, Karl Johans Gate, and Studenterlunden, the area which in many ways constitutes the heart of the city. Both newspapers are owned by Schibsted Gruppen.

The exuberant entry space and highly articulated exterior entrance celebrate the arrival at the headquarters of these two important newspapers. Although the vertically-shaped cylinder entry space defines a corner entry, an asymmetrical arrangement in massing and facades relates appropriately to the two streets on which it is located. The facade along Akersgaten is given a rich, horizontal expression in glass and steel, respectful of the height and character of the Government Building opposite. The long facade facing the side street, Apotekergaten, has a more complex copper-glass-stone-concrete treatment appropriate for its more intimate character. The entry cylinder pulls the two facades together by allowing vertical and horizontal elements and enclosed spaces to intersect and move through it. Along Teatergaten and Munch's Gate the building masses are pulled out as individual blocks or "walls." The separation of the two building blocks allows them to be rented out separately from the main part of the complex.

The centre of this unusual and idiosyncratic building site is defined by a large cylindrical atrium. Within this cylinder is suspended a floating cube, that houses the main staff cafeteria at the top from where there is a magnificent view of the entire City of Oslo. The cube is structurally supported by two asymmetrically placed columns, with an elevator on a slant attached to one of them. A diagonal walkway on the ground floor connects the main entrances at the corner of Akersgaten/Apotekergaten and the corner of Teatergaten/Munch's Gate, while intersecting the central cylindrical atrium. The articulated exterior facades give the two newspapers a new image.

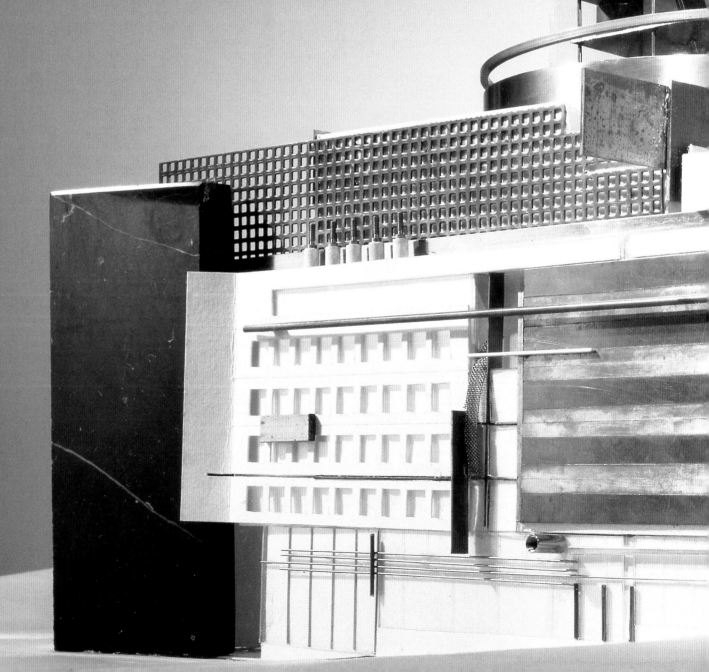

Schibsted Gruppen Newspaper Headquarters for Aftenposten and VG Oslo, Norway, 1989

Client: Schibsted Gruppen, Verdens Gang and Aftenposten:
Einar Fr Nagell-Erichsen
Alexandra Huitfelt
Stein Foyen
Erik Furevik
Kjell Aamot, VG
Geir Andersen, VG
Arne Tunheim, Aftenposten
Client Representative/Project Manager: Egil Vedal
Architect: Ellerbe Becket, New York
Peter Pran, Design Principal and Senior Vice President
Carlos Zapata, Senior Project Designer and Associate Design Director
B. Wayne Fishback, Senior Vice President, Administrative Principal
Curtis Wagner, Project Designer
Eduardo Calma, Project Designer
Vatche Asianian, Designer
Maria Wilthew, Project Designer
Robert Zumwalt, Chief Architect/Production
Michael Welebit, Project Manager
Model Photographer: Dan Cornish, ESTO
Associate Architect: Platou, Oslo, Norway
Jan Digerud, Partner
Jon Ronning, Partner
Henrik Arentzen, Technical Coordinator
Photographer: Dan Cornish

This project is the result of a carefully controlled juxtaposition of new functionally derived architectural elements over the structure of an existing Kevin Roche 1960s' building. The product is a sequence of elegant spaces enclosed among remaining structural corners and a sequentially located flowing layer of new architectural elements. Walls, partitions, lighting fixtures and furniture slide past one another without touching, in such a way as to give the space a sense of continuity and to allow natural light to filter from space to space. The procession from entry to back offices begins with a long glass reception desk supported by four curving steel ribs cantilevered from the floor. Above the desk is a long skylight that runs the entire length of the offices forming part of the original design of the building. All remaining elements are organized diagonally along the skylight attached to and suspended from floors, ceilings and walls, in order to create a well-balanced procession for the visitor. The choice of materials and the high quality of craftsmanship throughout create a forward-looking, sophisticated image. This project successfully incorporates many diverse uses including a TV studio, training facilities, management and client areas, a state-of-the-art reception area, board room and senior partner offices with support services.

Deloitte & Touche Headquarters Executive Area Wilton, Connecticut, USA, 1989

Client: Deloitte & Touche
Jerry Kolb, Vice Chairman and Chief Financial Officer
Gregory J. O'Connell, Manager, National Facilities
Architect: Ellerbe Becket, New York
Peter Pran, Senior Vice President and Design Principal
Carlos Zapata, Vice President and Associate Design Director
Ed Calma, Project Designer
B. Wayne Fishback, Administrative Partner
Carol Krewson, Project Director
Maria Wilthew, Designer
Curtis Wagner, Designer
Frank Yu, Designer
Michael Welebit, Project Manager
Arch Currie, Project Manager
Michael Rufino, Interior Designer
Moon Kim, Project Architect
Carol Napper
Ron Miranda
Photographers: Dan Cornish, Chuck Choi, Wayne Fuji

The new Psychiatric Institute is located on an exceptionally fine urban site west of Riverside Drive, and is connected to adjacent buildings in the Columbia Presbyterian Medical/ Research Complex via bridges across Riverside Drive. Laboratories are connected to the Kolb Annex Research Tower at the north end of the site; in-patient areas are connected to the Milstein Pavilion of Columbia Presbyterian Hospital at the south end. The prominent location of the site as one enters the city from the George Washington Bridge made a high-quality design addressing key urban design and community issues an imperative of the design process.

The building has magnificent views of the Hudson River, the George Washington Bridge and the north of Manhattan. The overall configuration maintains a low profile with a height of six stories above Riverside Drive allowing an open view corridor to the Hudson River from the neighbourhood around 168th Street pending the removal of the old NYPI building.

The new building allows public access in two locations: the main entry for automobiles located off Riverside Drive; pedestrians from the neighbourhood and from city transit locations at a higher elevation will enter via existing lobby space in the Kolb Research facility, with access to the new facility via the pedestrian bridge link. The entry on Riverside Drive is also formed by an open plaza, which leads into the existing natural landscape to the south of the building.

The overall building shape is defined by a laboratory research wing to the north and an in-patient and out-patient wing to the south. A dramatic six-storey atrium unifies the two wings and becomes the focal point of both grade and bridge circulation and orientation. The western facade takes the form of a gentle, curving wall which unites the two programmatic masses, gracefully defining its presence within the site. The curved exterior glass wall to the west reflects the flow of traffic along the West Side Highway, while the stepped eastern facades — in concrete, metal, and glass — along Riverside Drive define the arrival space and its specific urban spatial character. The dramatically different expressions of the west and east facades clearly reveal the site-specific qualities of the building.

In addition to laboratory research space, the new facility will house 72 in-patient psychiatric research beds, as well as a significant education and training component, a 24-bed community service in-patient unit, a public school for children being treated at the Institute, a state-of-the-art animal holding facility for transgenic mice, and administrative and support spaces. There is also a new power plant for the complex and a 100-car parking garage below the new building.

New York State Psychiatric Institute Manhattan, New York City, New York, USA, 1992-98

Client: New York Psychiatric Institute:
Dr. John Oldham, Director (and Chief Medical Officer for the State of New York)
Mr. Steven Papp, Director for Administration
Mr. Hal Seligson, Director of Business Office
Mr. Peter Reynolds, Director of Physical Plant
Ms. Ruth Corn, Director of Quality Assurance
Ms. Delores Kreisman, Director of Public Affairs
New York State Office of Mental Health (OMH):
Mr. Jim Stone, Commissioner for Office of Mental Health
Dr. Richard Surles, former Commissioner for Office of Mental Health
Mr. Skip Hommel, Director, Bureau of Capital Operations
Mr. David Beemer, Associate Director
Ms. Norma Roca, Facilities Coordinator & Manager (formerly Development Administrator with FDC)
Dormitory Authority: State of New York
Thomas Murphy, Chairman
John Buono, Executive Director
New York State Governors: Mario Cuomo (former), George Pataki (present)
Architects: Ellerbe Becket, New York
Peter Pran, Design Principal, Senior Vice President
Jill Lerner, Project Director/Managing Principal, Senior Vice President
Timothy Johnson, Senior Project Designer
Curtis Wagner, Designer
Dave Rova, Project Architect-Construction Documents
Lyn Rice, Designer
Bill Kidd, Senior Medical Planner
Don Velsey, Senior Medical Planner
Xenia Urban, Senior Medical Planner
Laura Ettelman, Project Architect
Jim Chin, Project Architect
Mike Jones, Managing Principal in later phase only
Al Zgolinski, Construction Supervision
Consulting Design Principal during construction: Peter Pran, NBBJ
Engineers: Seelye Stevenson, Value and Knecht, New York:
George Nagelberg, Chief Engineer and Principal
Construction and Construction Management: HRH/Hill
Joel Silverman, President
Frank Ross, Chairman
Bruce Fox, Administration P. E., Vice President, Chief Administrator
Raymond Martin, Project Manager
Jim Chin, Manager and Construction Supervisor
Richard Nichels, Project Director
Laboratory Consultants: GPR, New York:
Steve Rosenstein, Partner
Environmental Consultant: Ethan C. Eldon Associates:
Ethan Eldon, Principal
Photographers: Dan Cornish, Peter Pran, Timothy Johnson.
Photos by Dan Cornish were commissioned by Peter Pran

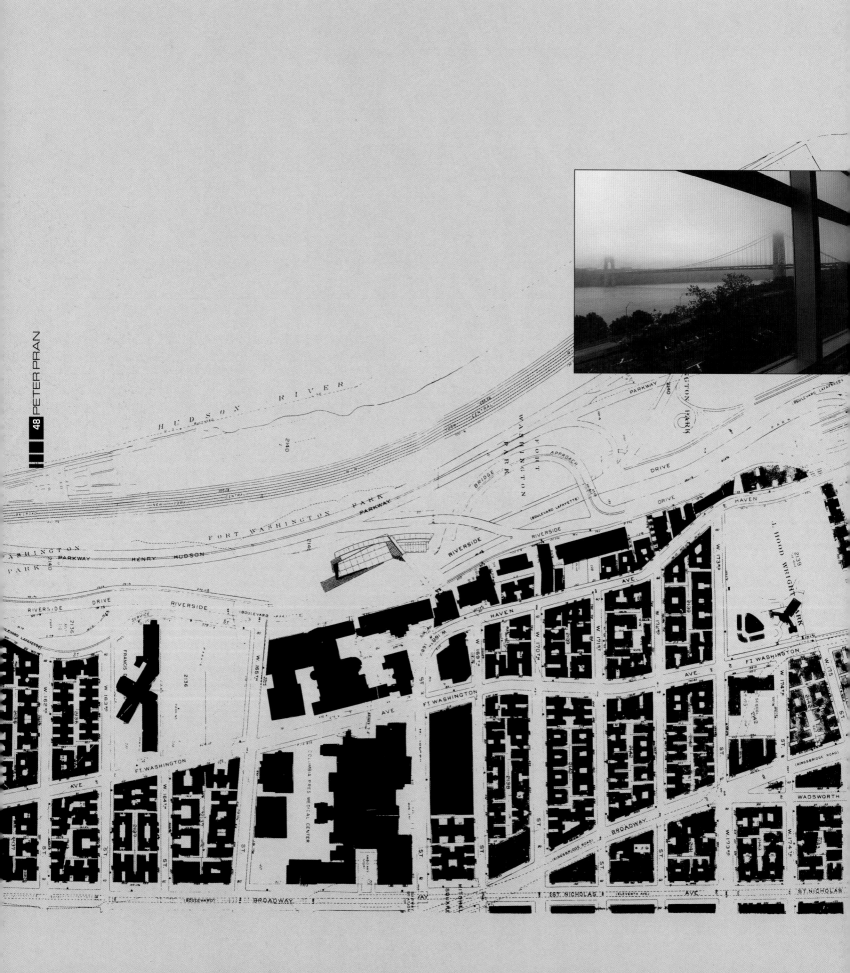

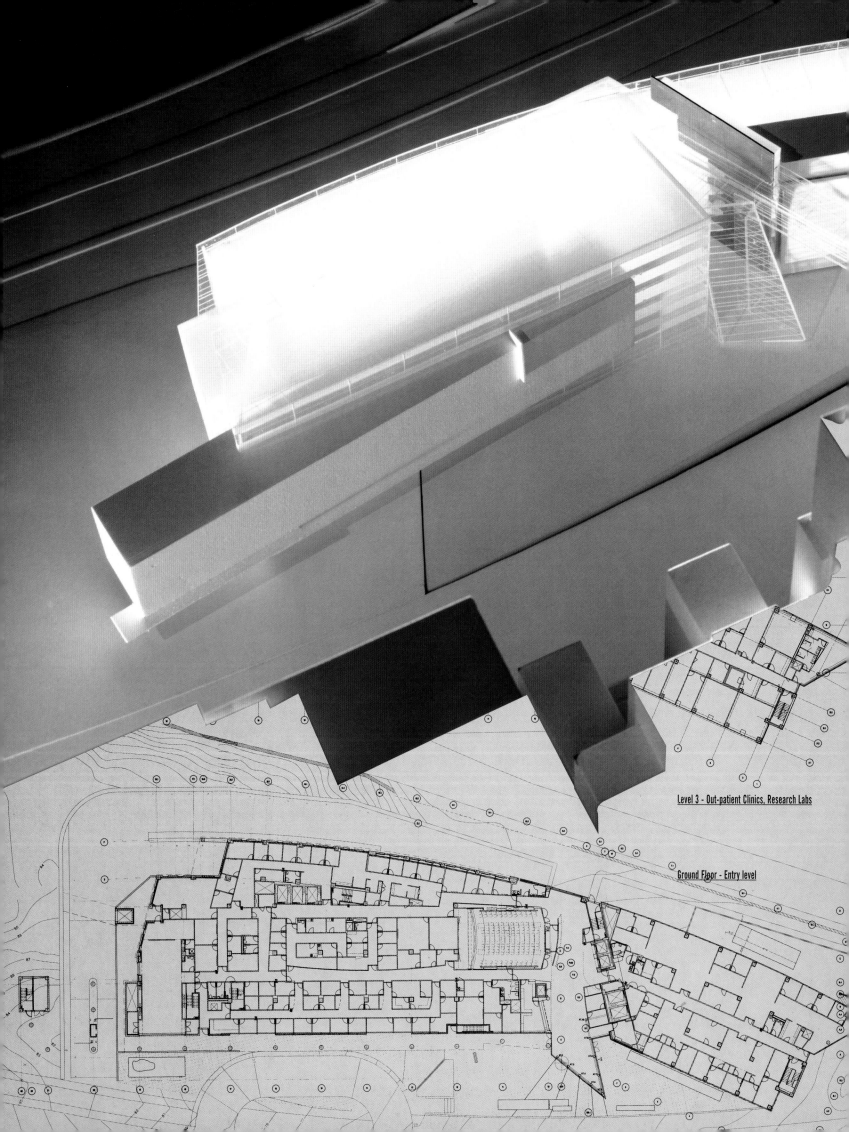

Level 3 - Out-patient Clinics, Research Labs

Ground Floor - Entry level

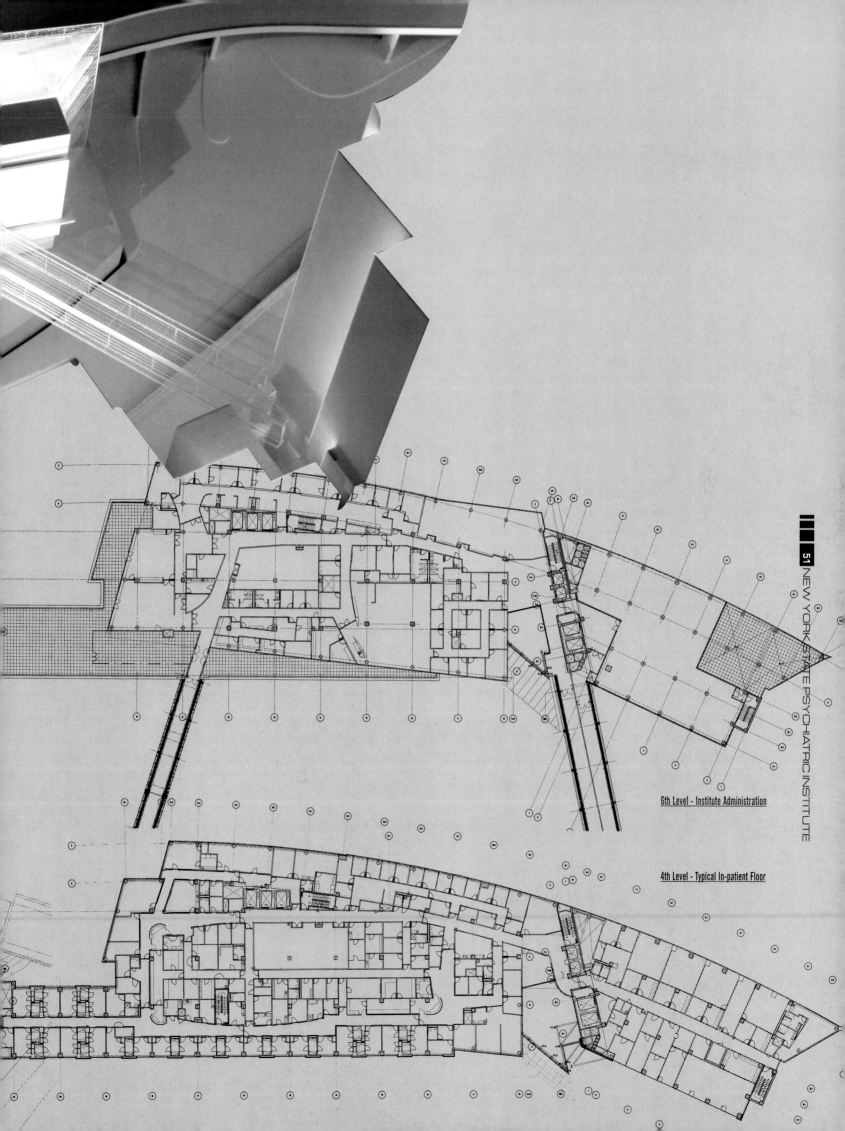

6th Level - Institute Administration

4th Level - Typical In-patient Floor

Bin Laden Corporate Headquarters Building Jeddah, Saudi Arabia, 1992

This new 90,000 sq.m headquarters for a major Saudi Arabian corporation is located on a magnificent site on the Red Sea, along the Corniche Boulevard, in Jeddah. The high-rise complex accommodates office space for 2,500 employees, a garage for 2,000 cars, and special amenities including a mosque. It provides an excellent environment for both staff and visitors. At the same time, the new building design concept gives a new and dignified image, representative of the company and the Kingdom of Saudi Arabia on the eve of the twenty-first century.

The high-rise complex consists of two vertical wings enclosing a beautiful, full height atrium. The building wing facing the Red Sea and the Corniche has the sail-like form of a gentle curve. The inside face of the curve gives the atrium a graceful, exuberant quality. The rectangular inlaid wing serves as a foil for this dramatic curve. The design is respectful of and appropriate for the city of Jeddah and at the same time of the highest international quality.

The client explicitly wanted a landmark building and feels that this innovative, original high-rise design meets that goal.

Client: Saudi Bin Laden Group, Jeddah, Saudi Arabia
Sheikh Bakr Bin Laden, Chairman
Sheikh Saleh Bin Laden
Samir F. Ataya, Manager
Architect: Ellerbe Becket Minneapolis and New York
Peter Pran, Design Principal
Ted Davis, Senior Project Designer
Tim Johnson, Senior Designer
Jeff Walden, Senior Designer
Pat Bougie, Project Architect
William D. Chilton, Project Manager
Scott Saunders, Structural Engineer
Brian Benson, Mechanical Engineer
Tom Crew, Electrical Engineer
David Loehr, Planner
Doug Renier, Civil Engineer
Photographer: Dan Cornish

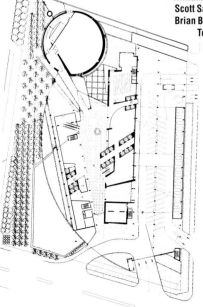

Ground Floor Plan

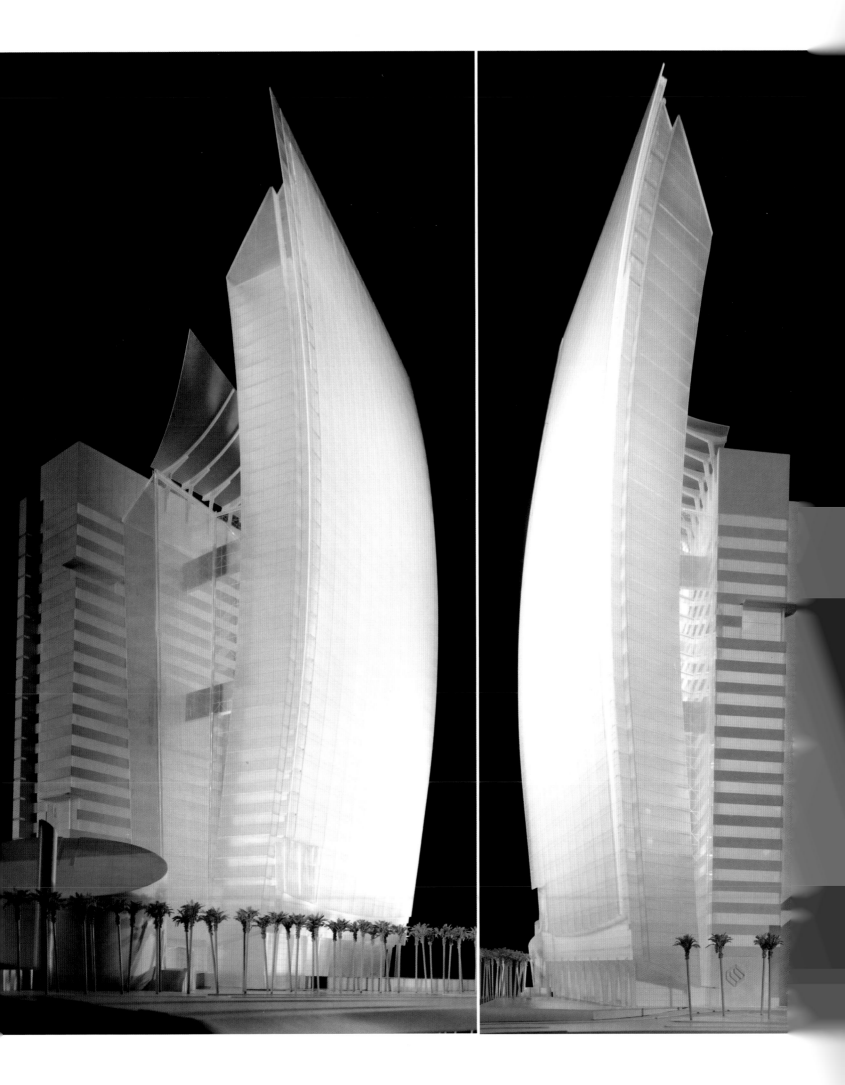

The commission was to design a 130,000 sq.ft. new academic facility for the State University of New York at Binghamton in upstate New York. The building serves as the new main entrance and "pedestrian gateway" to the campus from the main parking areas. It houses SUNY Binghamton's School of Management, School of Nursing, School of Education and Human Development, Academic Computing Centre, Research Programmes, Undergraduate Admissions, shared Lecture Hall and Classrooms. Furthermore, it creates a new image for a university that is emerging as one of the leading liberal arts institutions and one of the five top public universities nationally.

The selected two-building scheme, which is three stories high, fits in with the existing three-storey buildings on campus (the main height throughout), and provides the desired exterior identity to the different departments. An interior connection between the new and the existing buildings further integrates the project and becomes part of SUNY Binghamton's "winter campus" walkway. Building A contains mainly the School of Management and Undergraduate Admissions; and Building B contains mainly the School of Education and Human Development in its western wing and the School of Nursing in its eastern wing. The two atriums in Buildings A and B create the gateway to the entire campus; their varied tilts create a positive tension in the gateway.

The entry to the Admissions Office, shared Lecture Halls and Classrooms is at Building A's curved tip, in its atrium, which serves as the "gateway" point. The existing campus is dominated by a series of rectangular buildings on a 90 degree grid. The two new buildings break the grid to create a dynamic and friendly expression of movement and freedom in its architectural statement. The large metal roof at the large Lecture Hall comes out of the ground, with its interior hall relating to both first and ground floors. The buildings will continue the concrete, tile and colour palette of the existing neighbouring science buildings and at the same time add copper, stainless steel and stone to give a material richness.

The goal of the client was to design within tight budgetary constraints a complex that fits in with the campus but also brings in a new spirit and new high-quality architecture.

Client: Binghamton University, Binghamton, New York, and State University Construction Fund (SUCF) for the State University of New York at Binghamton (SUNY):
Lois de Fleur, President
Michael Scullard, Vice President
Larry Roma, Assistant Vice President, Facilities
Gene Gilliand, Assistant Vice President, Facilities
Gary Roodman, Acting Dean, SOM
Linda Biemer, Dean SEHD
Mary S. Collins, Dean SON
Geoff Gould, Admissions Fred Brooks, Enrollment
(SUCF) Bob Ruckterstuhl, Manager of Design

New Academic Buildings
State University of New York at Binghamton
Binghamton, New York, USA, 1991-98

Jim Biggane, Director of Consultant Design
Daryl Andreades, Associate Project Coordinator (SUNY)
Architect: Ellerbe Becket, New York
Peter Pran, Design Principal and Senior Vice President
Jill Lerner, Senior Vice President and Project Director
Lyn Rice, Project Architect/Designer
Carlos Zapata, Senior Designer and Vice President
Curtis Wagner, Project Designer
Eduardo Calma, Project Designer
Maria Wilthew, Designer
Timothy Johnson, Project Designer
Construction Documents and Construction Supervison:
Phil Rubin, Senior Project Architect and Vice President
Robert Zumwalt, Vice President and Project Manager
Robert Peralta, Project-Management
Brian McFarland, Computer Director
Diane Hayes, Interiors
Helen Ferguson, Designer
Gabriella Stamate, Technical
Joe Miou, Senior Technical Coordinator
Milton McCall, Technical
Louis Rivera, Technical
Kelly Vandeplasse, Technical
Mike Jones, Educational Planning,
Vice President and Design Principal
Structural Engineer: Les Robertson, New York
Saw-Teen See, Partner
Mechanical/Electrical Engineers:
Flack + Kurtz Engineers, New York
David Cooper
Tony Battaglia
Landscape Architect:
Office of William Kuhl
Civil Engineer: Ysrael Seinuk, PC
Photographers: Dan Cornish,
Maria Ryan Wagner
Photos by Dan Cornish were
commissioned by Peter Pran

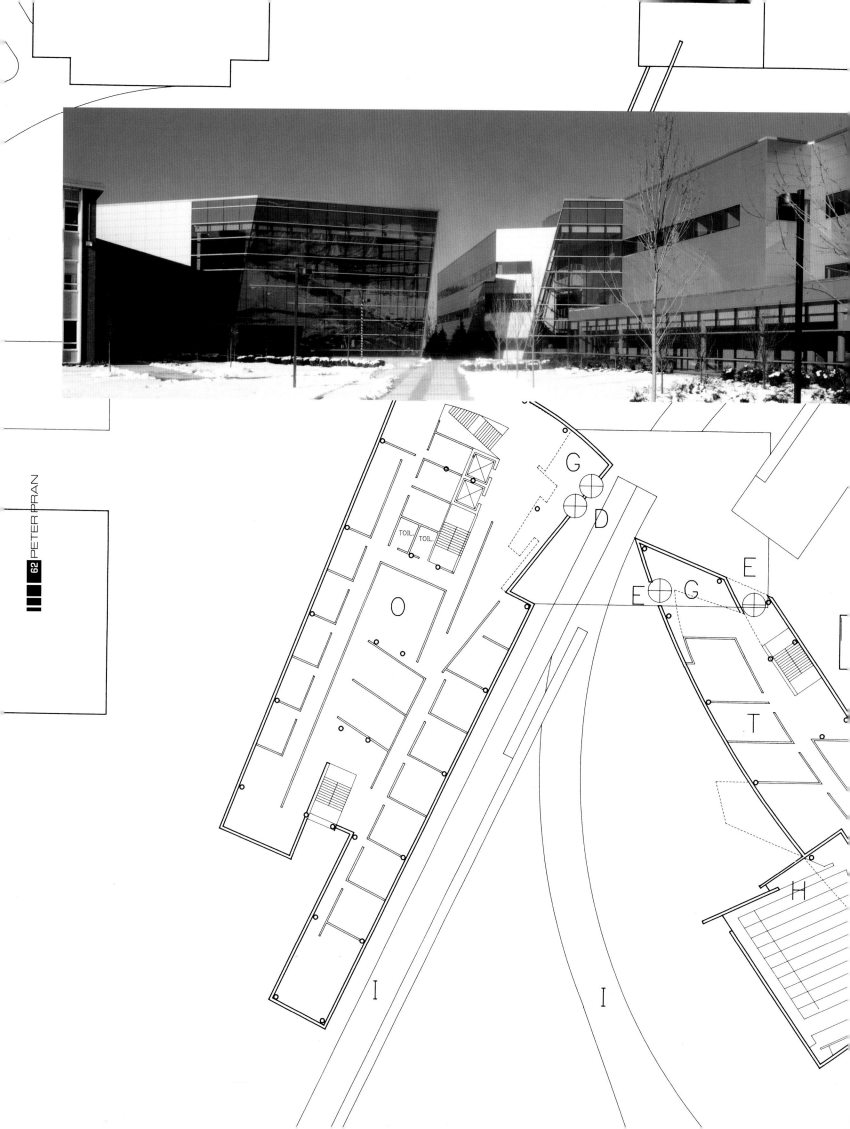

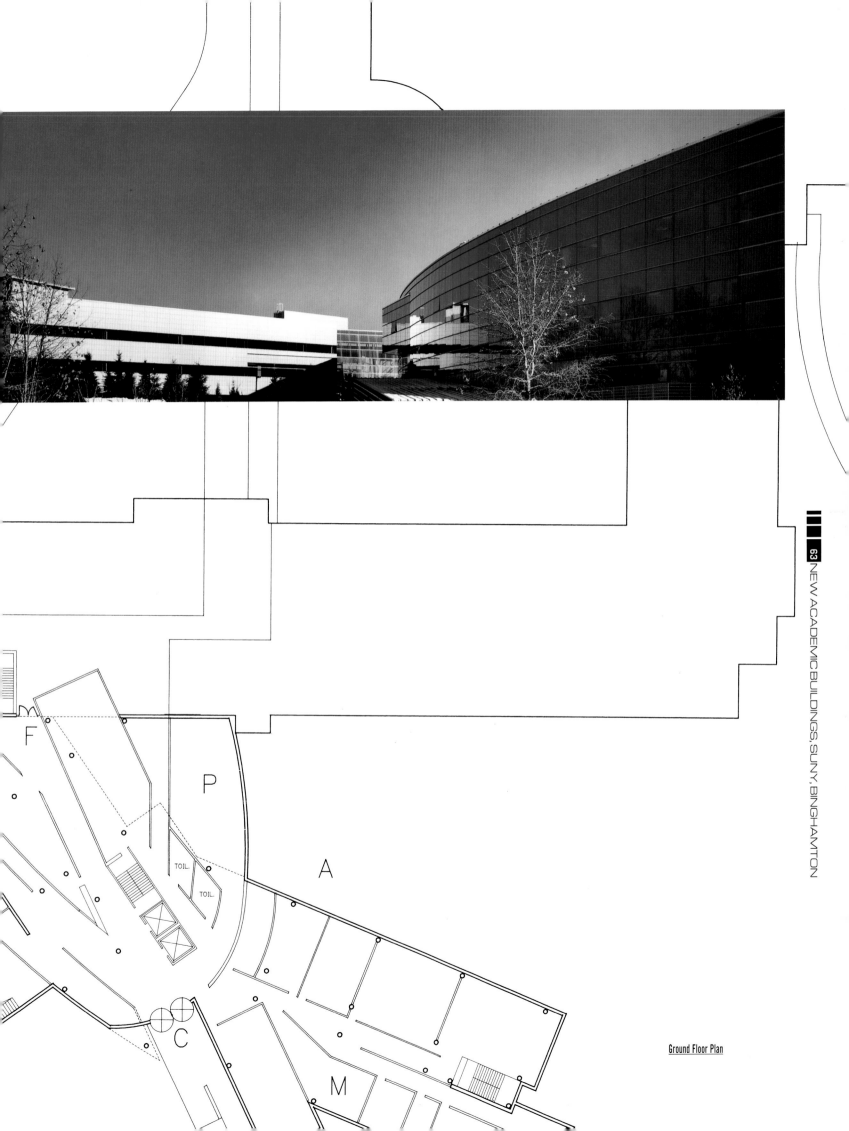

F

P

TOIL.

TOIL.

A

C

M

Ground Floor Plan

New York Police Academy Bronx, New York City, New York, 1993

This winning design in an international competition for a new police academy encompasses three main characteristics. Firstly, the ease with which it is operated and maintained; secondly, the support that the facility offers its users in their operations and daily routine; and, thirdly, its innovative architecture based on the recognition of the immeasurable impact the physical environment has on the well-being of its occupants. One of the aims was to develop innovative architectural ideas, coupled with good design to generate an invigorating new architecture into the area so that it becomes the beacon for a new standard.

Two grids (or armatures) were established and translated into two axes: axis one, academic spaces; and axis two, physical training spaces. Mediating between the precision of these two axes is a series of support elements which have programmatically connected to both axes and, in places, to public or visitor interaction. This includes administration and its symbolic role in directing all activities — mind and body related, as well as a series of special, more imposing spaces which include the museum, the auditorium and the library. The image of the building has succeeded in developing strength and movement in its architectural expression, while maintaining clarity of movement in and around the complex, so that the ease of use and fluid character of the various components heighten the awareness of an enduring, dignified image befitting the seriousness of law enforcement.

The winning design in the international invited architecture competition, competing with Norman Foster, Robert Venturi, Rafael Viñoly, Ed Larrabee Barnes.

Client: City of New York, New York Police Department, Bronx Borough
Architect: Ellerbe Becket, New York
Peter Pran, Design Principal, Senior Vice President
Paul Davis, Lead Senior Project Designer
Timothy Johnson, Senior Project Designer
Ed Calma, Project Designer
Andy Cers, Project Architect
Denny Wallace, Project Manager
Architect: Michael Fieldman & Partners
Michael Fieldman, Design Partner
Miles Cigolle, Associate Partner
Ed Rawlings, Project Architect
Andrew Heidig, Designer
Roger Goodhill, Designer
Elissa Icso, Designer
John Jordan, Project Architect
Jyh-Meei Jong, Designer
Structural Engineering: LERA
Les Robertson, Partner
MEP: Cosentini
Marvin Mass, Senior Partner
Graphics: Massimo Vignelli
Landscape Architecture: Paul Friedberg & Partners
Cost Consultants: Federman Construction Consultants
Model Builder: Richard Tenguerian
Photography: Dan Cornish

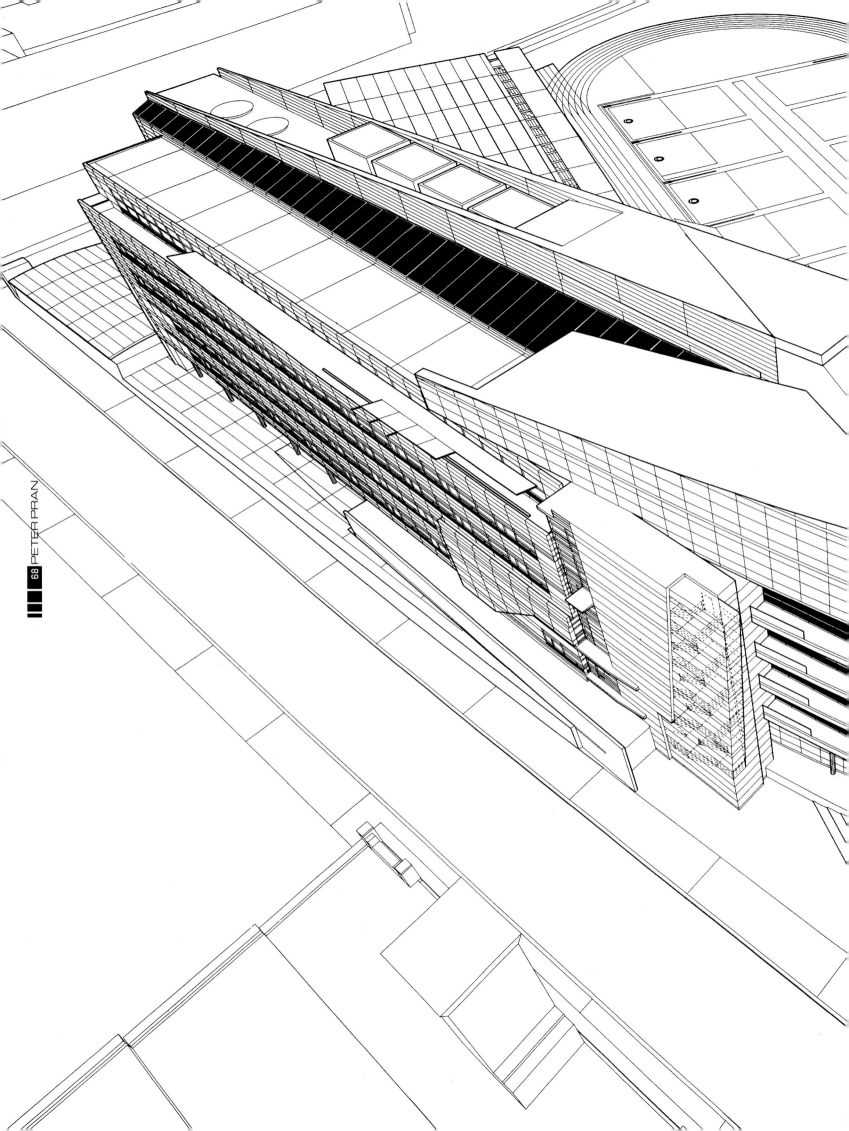

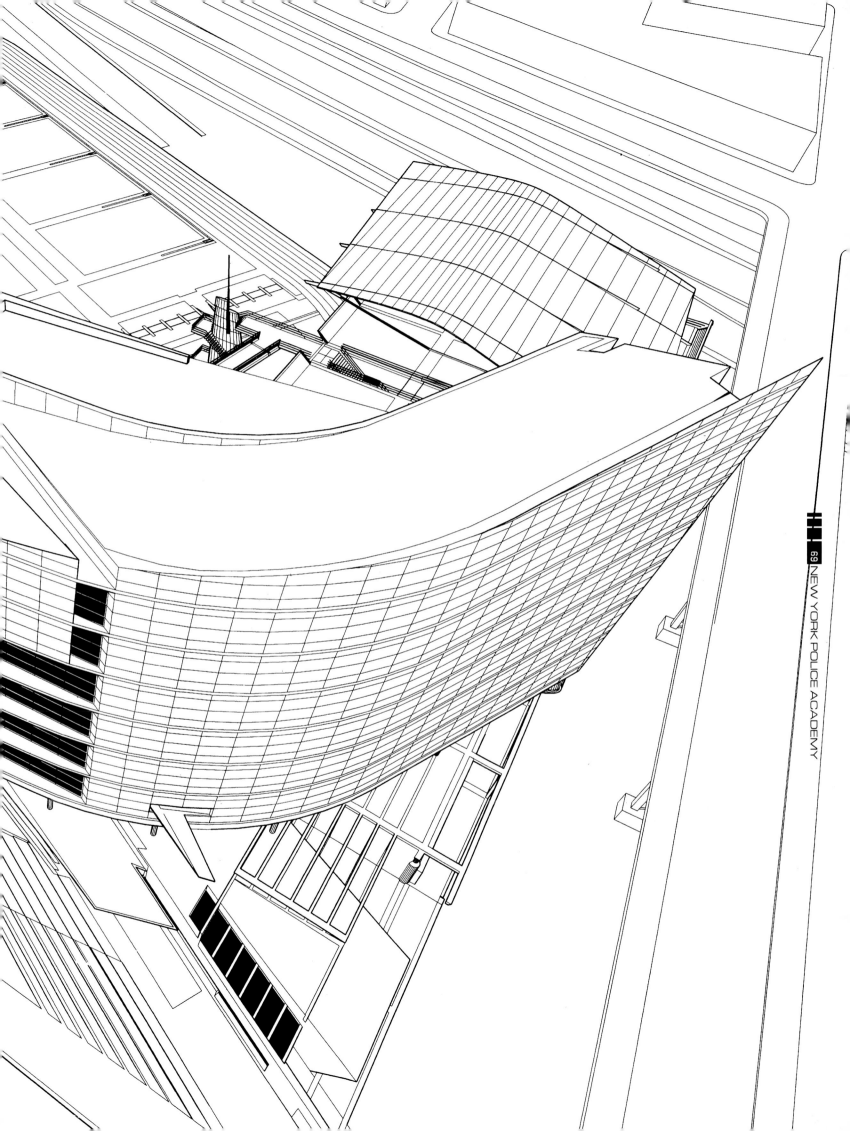

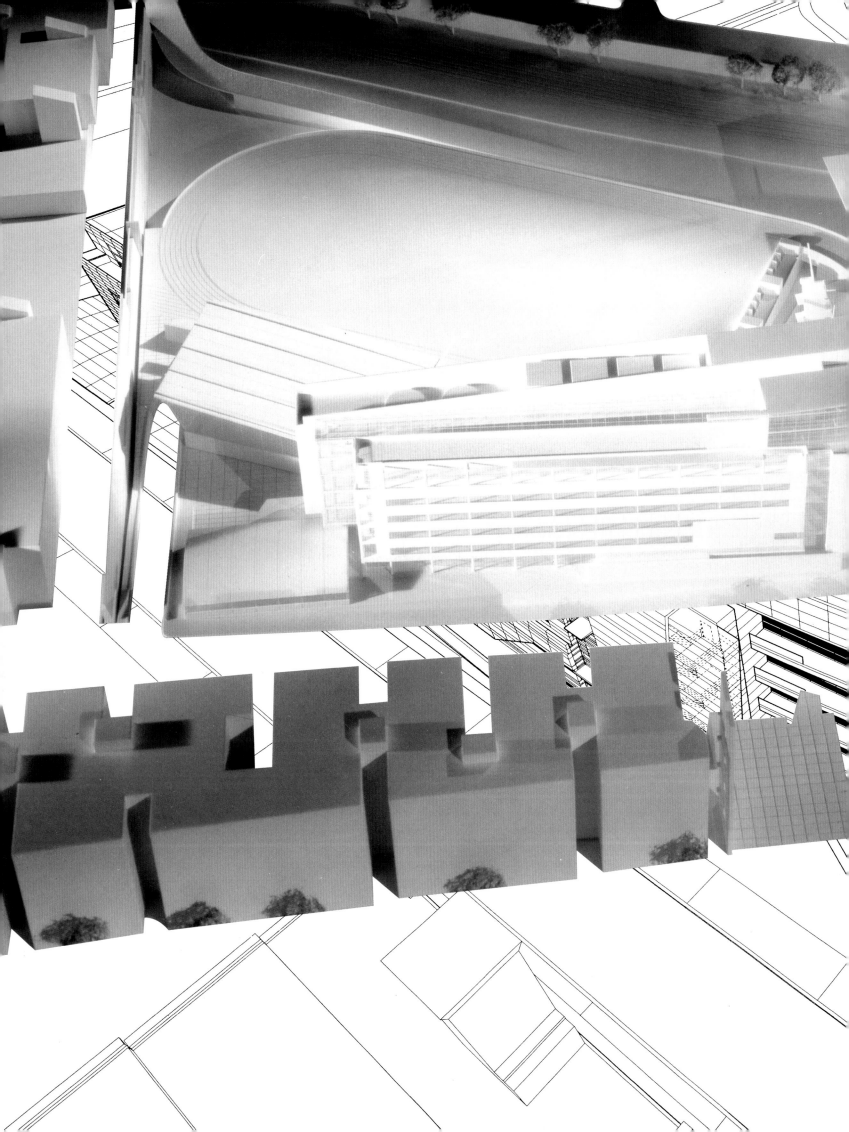

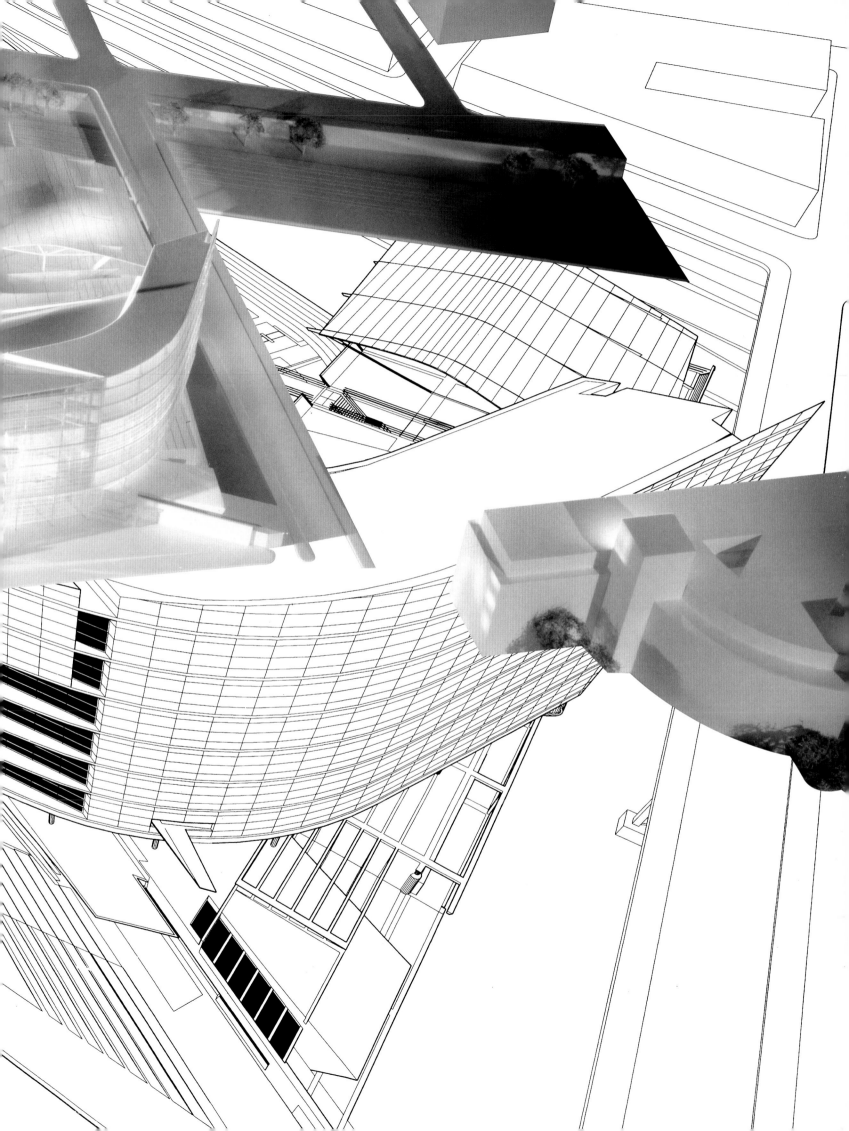

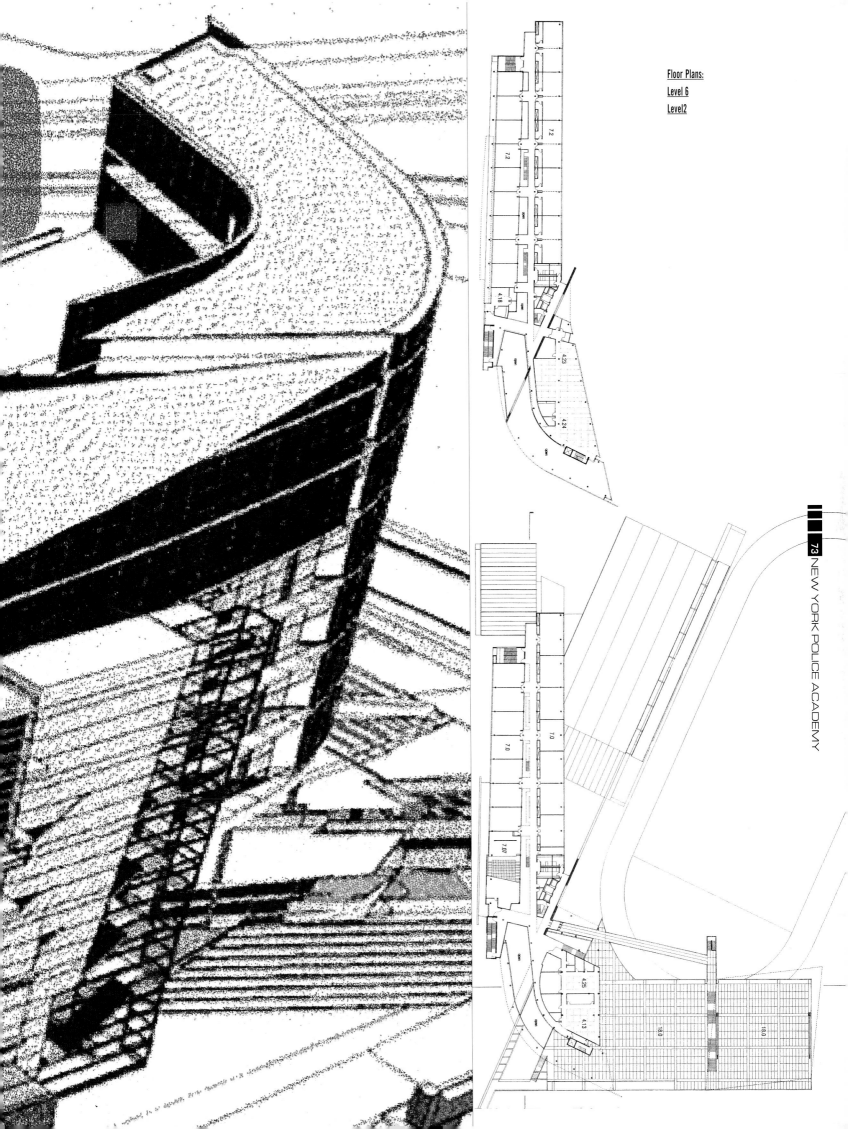

Floor Plans:
Level 6
Level2

Typical Low-rise Unit
Level 5 - Terrace
Entry Level

SOUTH POINT TOWER

Portofino Diamond C
Apartment Tower
Miami, Florida, USA, 1994

This mixed-use condominium tower complex located at the southernmost tip of Miami Beach with outstanding views of the Atlantic Ocean to the east and the shipping port and CBD area of downtown Miami to the west is a 40-storey residential high-rise, with five-storey low-rise base of parking and service amenities. It was designed to meet the client's desire for a modern apartment complex that would enhance the value and image of the area of by becoming an immediate architectural landmark.

The main tower mass, with its rectangular floor plan oriented in the long axis, is positioned to capture the dramatic views to west and east. The west facade resembles a sail in full breeze as it gently curves outwards in section as one ascends vertically. This facade, clad in floor to ceiling glass, expresses the building's residential programme through the tectonic layering of enclosure and structure, permitting the introduction of balconies and semi-enclosed *brise-soleil* while maintaining the overall building shape.

Recreational support facilities, including a health club with swimming pool, sun deck and tennis courts, are located in the building podium. A dynamic curved retail podium continues the rich art deco street fabric along Biscayne Street grounding the complex in the urban context.

Architect: Ellerbe Becket New York Office
Peter Pran, Design Principal
Timothy Johnson, Senior Project Designer
Jonathan Ward, Senior Project Designer
Maria Wilthew, Designer
Ed Calma, Designer
Carmine Marullo, Plan Consultant
Frank Mendoza, Graphic Coordinator
Lois Pezzi, Interiors
Ramesh Desai, Structural Engineer
Dennis Wallace, Project Manager
Model Maker: Richard Tenguerian, New York
Photography: Dan Cornish, Connecticut

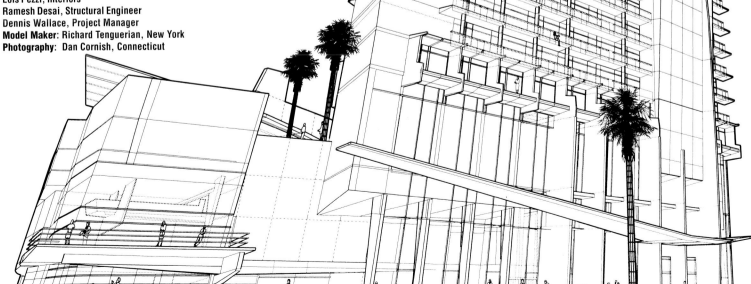

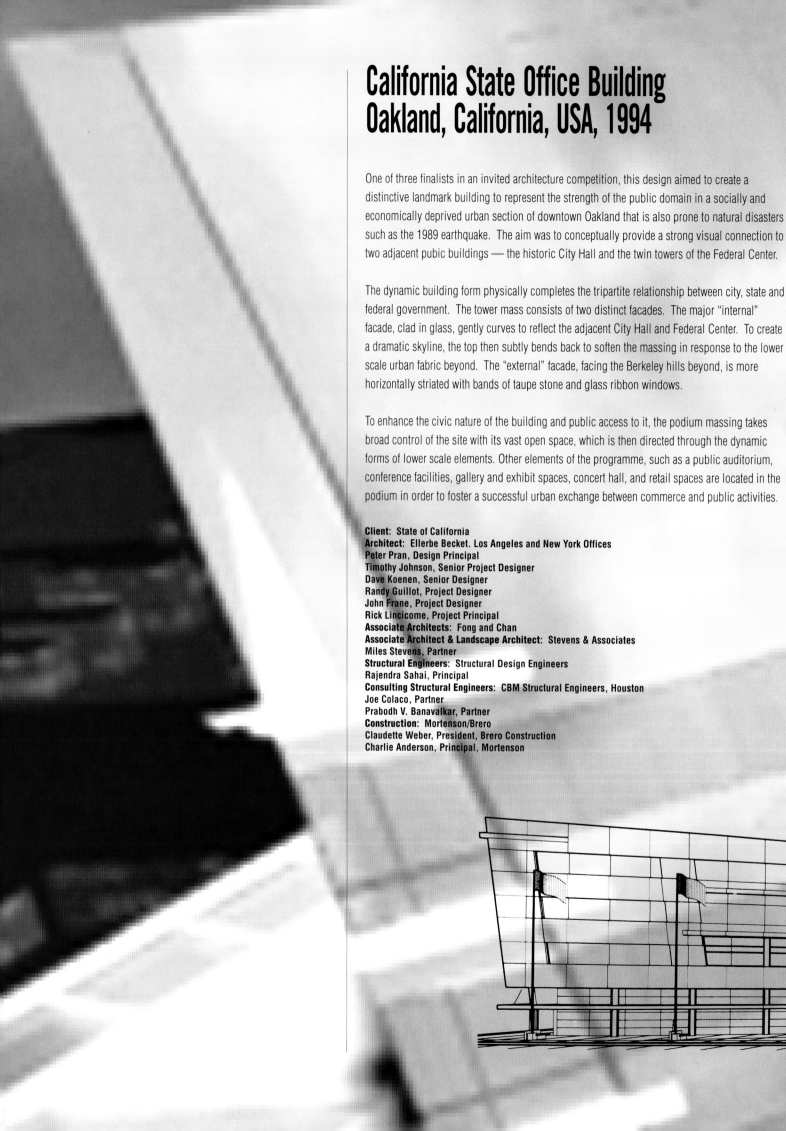

California State Office Building Oakland, California, USA, 1994

One of three finalists in an invited architecture competition, this design aimed to create a distinctive landmark building to represent the strength of the public domain in a socially and economically deprived urban section of downtown Oakland that is also prone to natural disasters such as the 1989 earthquake. The aim was to conceptually provide a strong visual connection to two adjacent pubic buildings — the historic City Hall and the twin towers of the Federal Center.

The dynamic building form physically completes the tripartite relationship between city, state and federal government. The tower mass consists of two distinct facades. The major "internal" facade, clad in glass, gently curves to reflect the adjacent City Hall and Federal Center. To create a dramatic skyline, the top then subtly bends back to soften the massing in response to the lower scale urban fabric beyond. The "external" facade, facing the Berkeley hills beyond, is more horizontally striated with bands of taupe stone and glass ribbon windows.

To enhance the civic nature of the building and public access to it, the podium massing takes broad control of the site with its vast open space, which is then directed through the dynamic forms of lower scale elements. Other elements of the programme, such as a public auditorium, conference facilities, gallery and exhibit spaces, concert hall, and retail spaces are located in the podium in order to foster a successful urban exchange between commerce and public activities.

Client: State of California
Architect: Ellerbe Becket. Los Angeles and New York Offices
Peter Pran, Design Principal
Timothy Johnson, Senior Project Designer
Dave Koenen, Senior Designer
Randy Guillot, Project Designer
John Frane, Project Designer
Rick Lincicome, Project Principal
Associate Architects: Fong and Chan
Associate Architect & Landscape Architect: Stevens & Associates
Miles Stevens, Partner
Structural Engineers: Structural Design Engineers
Rajendra Sahai, Principal
Consulting Structural Engineers: CBM Structural Engineers, Houston
Joe Colaco, Partner
Prabodh V. Banavalkar, Partner
Construction: Mortenson/Brero
Claudette Weber, President, Brero Construction
Charlie Anderson, Principal, Mortenson

Karet Office Tower
Jakarta, Indonesia, 1995

First Prize in an international design competition.

The design of the Karet Office Tower describes a progressive form on the skyline of Jakarta, responding to the dynamics of the modern city. It marks its prominent urban position within Jakarta's Golden Triangle through the composition of pure, abstract forms and lines. The project consists of two components: a 40-storey (60,000 sq.m) office tower, and a detached 10-storey (30,000 sq.m) parking structure which is connected to the office tower via sky bridges.

The design has two distinct facades: one oriented to Jalan Jeneral Sudirman (the main thoroughfare of Jakarta's CBD), which is a glass slab with a dramatically curved top that responds to the urban city scale and iconic qualities of the CBD; and a west facade, which is approached upon entry to the tower, responding to the scale and forces of the low-rise urban fabric of this location. This western facade, composed of a series of horizontal glass and metal panel plates, is subtly curved in plan creating a dynamic movement towards the corner intersection of the site.

In plan, the rectilinear floor plate of the office tower efficiently utilizes a common central core which allows quadrant sub-divisions with little excess circulation space. In addition, the creation of multiple corner office configurations through the shifting composition of the two-sided mass creates rich office planning opportunities. As the mass runs vertically, the straightforward plan then begins to decrease, giving way to the curved section penthouse floors.

The design successfully balances the basic needs of the typical tenant and the financial requirements of the developer, while creating a strong and powerful image for the tenants and the city of Jakarta.

Client: PT Duta Anggada
Hartadi Ankosubruta, President
Widijanto, Director
Architect: Ellerbe Becket New York Office (S.D + D.D.)
Peter Pran, Design Principal
Jonathan Ward, Senior Project Designer
Timothy Johnson, Project Designer
David Rova, Project Architect/Manager
Mark Goldstien, Designer
Ana O'Brien, Designer
Marius Radeleceau, Designer
Architect: P.T. Califa Pratama (C.D. + C.A.)
Timothy Hadiwibawa
Consulting Design Principal: Peter Pran of NBBJ (C.D. + C.A.)
Consulting Structural Engineers: Wong, Hobach, Lau
Francis Lau, Partner
Consulting Mechanical Engineers: P.T. Arnan Pratama

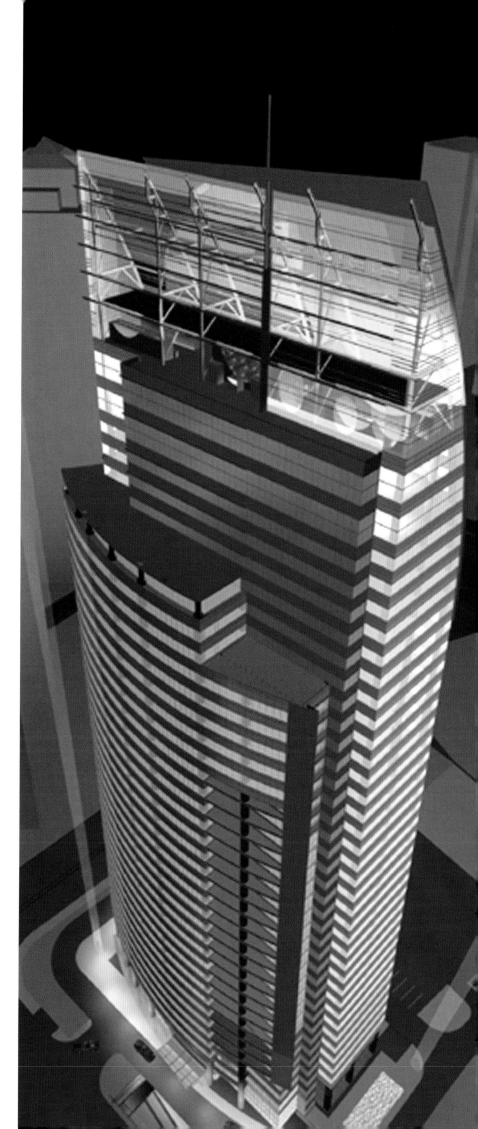

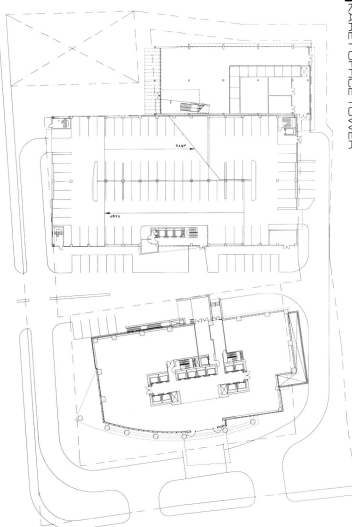

Graha Kuningan
Jakarta, Indonesia, 1995-98

Graha Kuningan wih its 50-storey (70,000 sq.m) commercial office building and 4-storey (10,000 sq.m) retail and entertainment podium is prominently located along Jakarta's Golden Triangle.

The office tower mass consists of two curving arcs shifted in plan to create a vertically slender, dynamic building form. Its enclosure of reflective aqua-green glass is further articulated with aluminium mullion fins giving the mass a distinct aerodynamic feel. This horizontal expression emphasizes the taut, machined nature of the thin glass plane. The top of the building is stepped down on the northern face to further articulate the shifted facades, and to create an outdoor terrace at the 47th level penthouse floor. Internally, the central core runs nearly the entire length of the long axis and is narrowly configured to maximize office layout and planning opportunities. The exterior glazing affords outstanding panoramic views of the city.

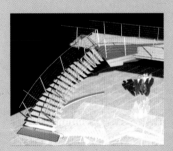

The podium with its services and support functions provides an internal, self-sustaining environment in keeping with business and entertainment in Jakarta.

The building, due for completion for the year 2000, will be the world's 77th tallest building.

Cross Section

Client/Owner/Developer: P.T. Pacific MetroRealty (PMR)
Suhadi Zaini, President Director
Prajogo Pangestu, Vice Chairman
Budi Ishak, Director
Djatikesumo Subagio, Manager
Mutyadewi Subagio, Manager
Coki Syaiff, Designer
Susanto Hardjoko, Manager
Design Consultant through CD (revised and redone) and Construction: NBBJ
Peter Pran, Design Principal
Dorman Anderson, Managing Principal
Jonathan Ward, Senior Project Designer
John Pangrazio, Partner
Design Consultant through CD and Construction: Timothy Johnson
Former Architect: Ellerbe Becket, New York and Minneapolis (through SD, DD and partial CD)
Peter Pran, Design Principal
Paul Davis, Senior Project Designer
Jonathan Ward, Senior Project Designer
Timothy Johnson, Senior Project Designer
Dave Koenen, Project Designer
Guy Painchaud, Interior Designer
Tom Schneider, Project Manager
Dennis Wallace, Project Manager
Chris Mullen, Designer
Roger Goodhill, Designer
Hung Russel, Project Architect
Jean Garbarini, Landscape Designer
Bryan Carlson, Landscape Designer
Rollin Hansen, Manager
Steve Harbin, Construction Services
Doug Maust, Mechanical
Al Wenzel, Electrical
Interior Architects: Tony Chi and Paul Hsu, New York
Associate Architect/Architect of Record: Jasa Ferrie
Thomas Tirtha, Principal
Agustinus DS, Project Architect
Nugroho Widhi, Project Architect
Chairul Abri, Senior Architect
Architectural Coordination: Michael Lavery, Manager, Thomson Adsett, Australia
Model: Richard Tenguerian, New York
Structural Engineering: LERA/Leslie E. Robertson Associates, RLLP
Les Robertson, Partner
Bill Faschan, Partner
Monica Svojsik, Manager
Daniel Sesil, Partner
Saw-Teen See, Managing Partner
Associate Structural Engineer: P.T. Thomas Sardjono
Thomas Sardjono, Principal
Jodi Firmansjah, Designer
I. Wayan Sengara, Designer
F. Budiyasa Winato, Designer
Mechanical/Electrical Engineers: P.T. Meco Systech Internusa
Computer Model & 3D-Studio Graphics: Paul Davis, Dave Koenen, Derek McCallum, Joey Myers
SGI Renderings: Creaturework
Photographers: Dan Cornish, Peter Pran and Timothy Johnson
Quantity Surveyor: P.T. Korra Antarbuana
Curtain Wall: Albert Leung, Hong Kong
Vertical Transportation: Lerch Bates Associates, Littleton, Colorado
Contractor: Taisei

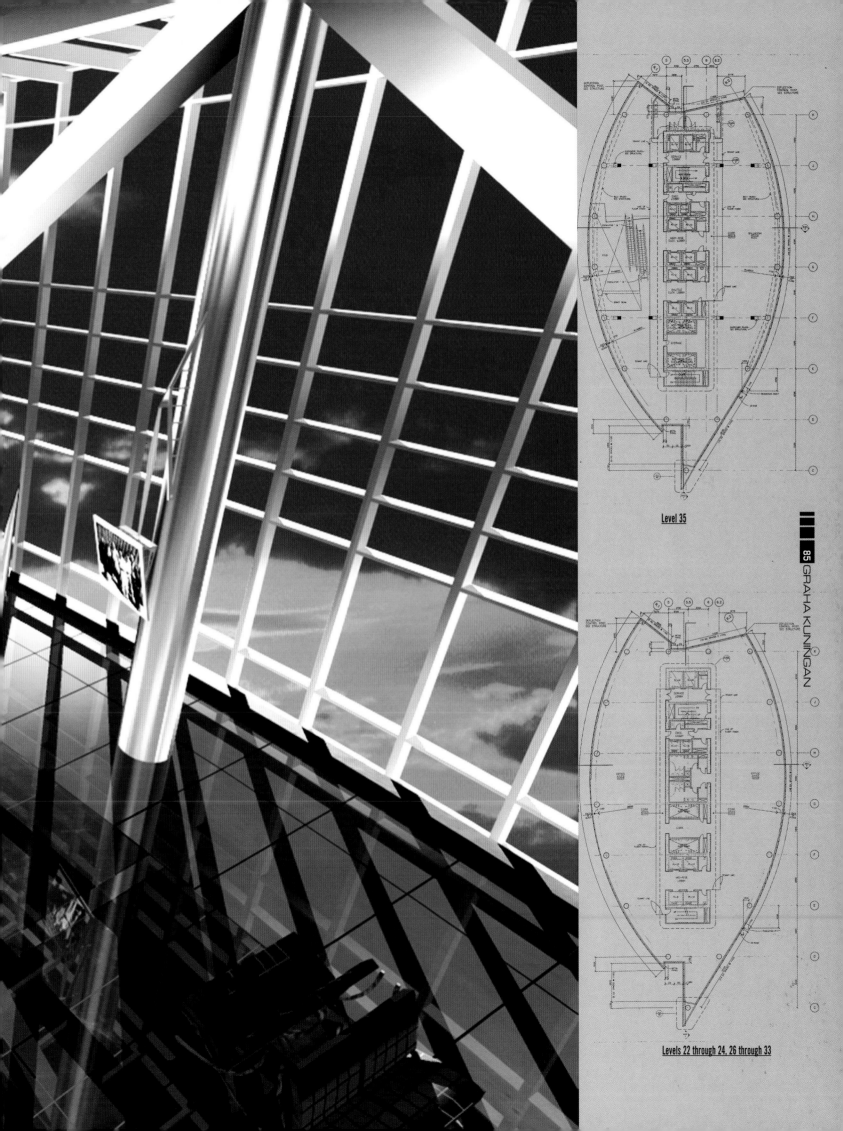

Level 35

Levels 22 through 24, 26 through 33

This executive floor provides a main boardroom/ conference room, a smaller conference room, individual offices for the board members, secretarial space, a large open work space for most staff, a marketing office area, and restrooms.

The interior layouts have an energy and a flow in an innovative modern setting. Tilted metal walls define the main board room and the arrival space for the individual offices for the board members; tilted, curved parallelogram doors swing open on two pegs and become part of the walls when the doors are closed. A rich use of stainless steel, copper, granite, marble and leather in the interiors gives a comfortable modern feel. The floor-to-ceiling glass ensures magnificent views.

PMR Executive Interiors, 21st Floor, Menara Imperium Jakarta, Indonesia, 1995-97

Client: P.T. Pacific MetroRealty
Suhadi Zaini, President Director
Djatikesumo Subagio, Manager
Mutyadewi Subagio, Manager
Coki Syaiff, Designer
Susanto Hardjoko, Manager
Architect: Ellerbe Becket New York
Peter Pran, Design Principal
Timothy Johnson, Senior Project Designer
Jonathan Ward, Designer
Guy Painchaud, Designer
Photos: Peter Pran, Timothy Johnson, Ahkamul Hakim

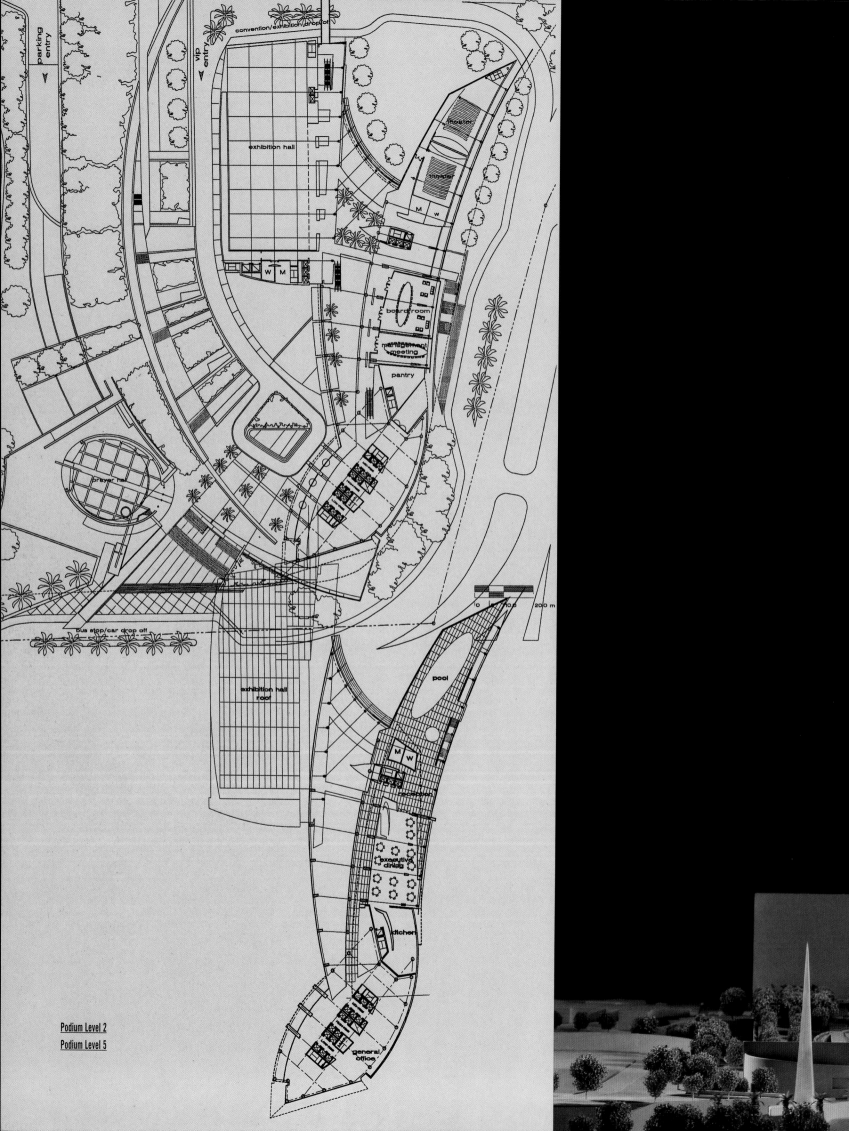

parking
entry

convention/exhibition drop off

vip
entry

exhibition hall

theater

theater

M   W

W   M

boardroom

management
meeting

pantry

prayer hall

bus stop/car drop off

0   100   200 m

exhibition hall
roof

pool

M   W

executive
dining

kitchen

general
office

Podium Level 2
Podium Level 5

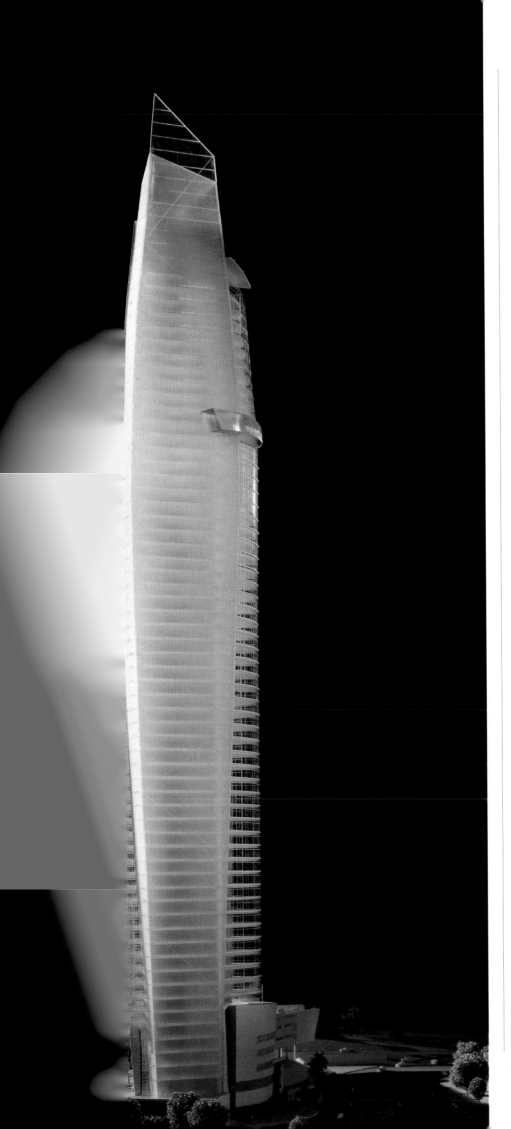

TNB Headquarters Tower
Kuala Lumpur
Malaysia, 1995

The TNB Office Tower was designed as part of an invited
architecture competition with five selected finalists to build a
new corporate headquarters for Tenaga Nasional Berhad, a
leading Malaysia commercial company. Other invited
architects included Jean Nouvel, Norman Foster, Helmut
Jahn and RTKL.

The project, part of an extensive master plan development, is
located just outside the main Kuala Lumpur CBD on the way
to the capital's international airport. It consists of a 60-storey
(70,000 sq.m) office tower and a complex of lower structures
including theatres, conference centre, exhibition hall, library,
mosque, executive centre and landscaping. These components are all linked via a dramatic atrium. The whole complex
is sited on top of a hill overlooking the city.

The design reflects aspects of Islamic values transformed into
modern architecture with modern technology. The tower itself
is composed of a series of atriums and sky gardens that
literally walk up the entire height of the building and open up
the modern office environment to exuberant vertical (and
horizontal) spatial experiences. The base of the building is a
rich combination of functions and spaces that weave into the
gardens below. Vertically, there is a dialogue between the two
distinct building masses in the tower.

The entire project was designed — with models and computer
drawings — in three weeks. This is typical of south-east
Asian projects where, although design time is limited, a
complete and convincing product must be presented.

Architect: Ellerbe Becket New York
Peter Pran, Design Principal
Jonathan Ward, Senior Project Designer
Timothy Johnson, Senior Project Designer
Dave Koenen, Project Designer
Lawrence Kim, Designer
Frank Mendoza, Graphic Coordinator
Architect in Kuala Lumpur: Focus Architects
Mohd Nazam Md Kassim, Director
Shah Sidek, Associate Director
Structural Engineer: Les Robertson, New York
Les Robertson, Partner
Bill Faschan, Partner
Saw-Teen See, Partner
Mechanical/Electrical Engineer: Syska & Hennesey
John Magliano, Partner
Lalit Mehta, Project Engineer
Model: Richard Tenguerian
Photographer: Dan Cornish

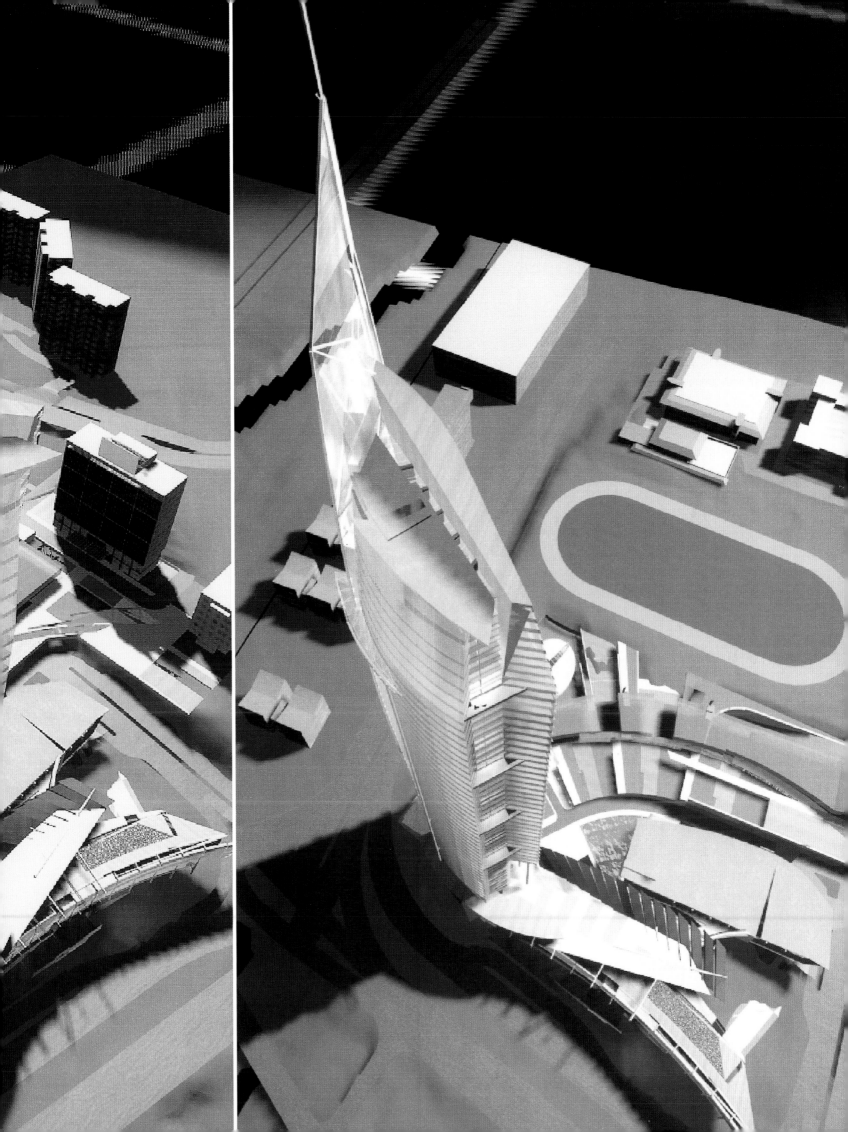

New Waterfront Development
Tip Top Tailor Building Complex
Toronto, Ont., Canada, 1995

This winning entry from five invited architects mainly retains
the existing building with the gentle intersection of a unifying
wedge-shaped interior/exterior atrium and a new horizontal
apartment and mixed-use wing that tie into the apartment
tower, which is a lit vertical accent along the waterfront.
The new and old buildings interweave rather than remaining in juxtaposition.

The renovated old building houses community facilities —
daycare centre, conference centre, small museum at
ground level, with offices above. Live-work spaces and
loft-style residential units are created within a gentle arc
slicing through Tip Top alongside the atrium, forming
outdoors the curved edge of a courtyard and plaza.

The project defines an invigorating dualism of old and
new, an appropriate addition to Toronto's attractive
waterfront.

Client: Dylex Limited
Architects: Ellerbe Becket, New York
Peter Pran, Design Principal
Timothy Johnson, Lead Senior Project Designer
Jeff Walden, Senior Project Designer
Dave Koenen, Project Designer
Denny Wallace, Manager
Quadrangle Architects, Toronto
Brian Curtner, Partner-in-charge
Roland Rom Colthoff
Ted Shore
Wyn Bielaska
D. Cusimano
W. Fritz
P. Goldsmith
B. Gordon
H. Hanson
L. Klein
C. Shear
G. Tassone
Structural Engineers: Yolles Partnership, Inc.
Landscape Architects: Ferris & Quinn Associates, Inc.
Development Consultants: Tanurb Developments
Marketing Consultants: The Carver Company
Construction Consultants: Vanbots Construction Corporation

Seoul Broadcasting Centre (SBS) Seoul, Korea, 1995

This competition entry for the Seoul Broadcasting System's new broadcasting centre is designed to develop an innovative, far-sighted architectural image with a rational functionality indicative of SBS as a new, young, progressive broadcast and media company.

The building is sited facing south towards Omok Park, establishing an overt relationship with the park and projecting an open image to the city. It consists of a 26-storey tower, SBS hall, and three large production studios in the base. SBS hall is a 1,000-seat auditorium which acts as a public filter for the image of SBS. The production facilities at the base are developed around spaces and movement of the staff.

The tower is a clear functional expression of its programme; the studios and technical functions are separated structurally and aesthetically from the more transparent form of the office and support spaces. The split between the two is resolved by the transmission tower at the peak of the building — its crowning expression.

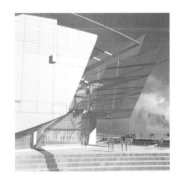

Client: Seoul Broadcasting System
Architect: Ellerbe Becket New York
Peter Pran, Design Principal
Jonathan Ward, Lead Senior Project Designer
Timothy Johnson, Senior Project Designer
Laura Ettelman, Project Architect
Dave Koenen, Project Designer
Maria Wilthew, Project designer
Rosette Khourenian, Designer
Frank Gunther, Project Manager
Kyun Kim, Project Director
Frank Mendoza, Graphic Coordinator
Associate Architects: Jung Lim, Seoul, Korea
Chang il Kim, Vice Chairman
Jin Goo Kim, Project Director
Engineering: Ove Arup, New York and Los Angeles
Mahadev Ramen, Mechanical Engineer
Richard Bussel, Acoustic Engineer
Matthew King, Structural Engineer
Stephen Pollard, Communications Engineering
David Richards, Mechanical Engineer
Broadcasting Consultant: National Telecom, Los Angeles
Charles Phelan, Managing Director
Robert Slutske, Vice President

Curitiba Arena, Hotel and Retail Centre
Curitiba, Brazil, 1996

The Curitiba Mixed-Use project has an arena, a large shopping centre, and a vertical 30-storey hotel. The arena will be used more for entertainment, concerts and exhibits than for sports events. The design of the complex is carefully adjusted to the softly curved site, and makes the streets and the neighbourhood come dramatically alive. This kind of multi-use sport and entertainment facility is popular in Brazil.

Clube de Regatas Flamengo/Flamengo Stadium
Rio de Janeiro, Brazil, 1995

The 23,000-seat Flamengo Stadium will be the home of the world-champion Brazilian soccer team. It will replace the existing open-air facility and is located at a prominent waterfront site in the city centre with prime views of the bay and the dramatic topography beyond.

Its dramatic curved roof, which covers the entire stadium, can be closed in ten minutes in the event of inclement weather, and allows the stadium to be fully air-conditioned during the hot season.

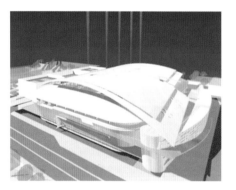

Architect: Ellerbe Becket New York Office
Peter Pran, Design Principal
Timothy Johnson, Senior Project Designer
Jonathan Ward, Senior Project Designer
Dave Koenen, Project Designer
Frank Gunther, Manager
Thom Greving, Planner
Architect: Coutinho, Diegues and Cordeiro, Rio de Janeiro
Antonio Paul Cordeiro, Partner
Anibal Coutinho, Partner

Mozadi Office Building
Jakarta, Indonesia, 1996

This 10-storey office building in downtown Jakarta has 10,000 sq.m of prime executive office space. The front facing exterior facade is tilted out at 8 degrees to maximize development potential. The top three levels, to be occupied by the owners, are accentuated by reversing the outward tilt to introduce a three-storey atrium in which the boardroom is suspended. A bridge over a sunken court defines the main entry.

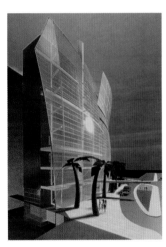

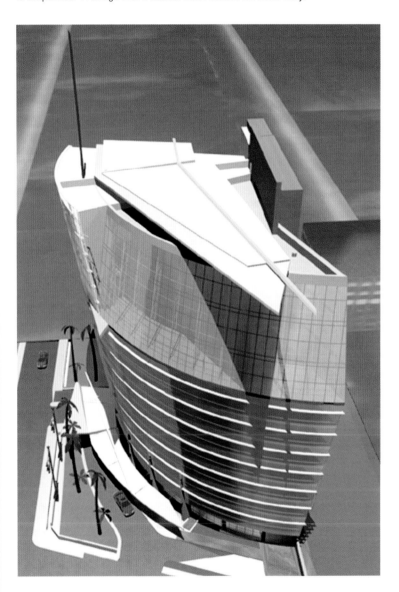

Architect: Ellerbe Becket New York
Peter Pran, Design Principal
Timothy Johnson, Lead Senior Project Designer
Jonathan Ward, Senior Project Designer
Dave Koenen, Senior Project Designer
Paul Davis, Senior Project Designer

80-Storey Mixed-Use Jakarta Tower
Jakarta, Indonesia, 1996

The winning design in an international invited architecture competition, this mixed-use project combines an 80-storey office and hotel tower with a 20-storey entertainment, retail, and parking podium. The site is located on the south-east tip of Jakarta's Golden Triangle, at a major street intersection, which has shaped the overall building complex in form, direction and movement.

Its prominent location makes the new building a focal point or gateway to the city. Its position, oriented diagonally on the site, gives it maximum visual exposure to vehicles approaching from four directions. The edge of the tower that points towards the intersection is tilted outwards two-thirds of the way up and curved back — in an oval plan — at the third upper portion so that it cuts with great ease through the surrounding layers of cloud and airstreams. It is hard not to imagine a ship sailing through space. From above, the tower interacts with the lower mass and the ground, anchoring the skyscraper to the city.

The bottom three floors with their hanging gardens and public open spaces, are designed to house the shopping centre's retail space. Two sets of lifts provide direct access to the sky-lobby, a spacious two-storey wing protruding out of the front of the skyscraper about two-thirds of the way up, providing a second entrance lobby for the remaining twenty-five floors of office space.

The lower building mass has an enormous ten-storey digital/electronic/high-tech screen with a constantly changing, highly luminous surface that delivers a form of non-stop visual communication made up of rapid sequences of designed media images. Electronic interaction with architecture is here to stay. In this building they work together.

Architect: NBBJ
Peter Pran, Design Principal
Jonathan Ward, Senior Project Designer
Dorman Anderson, Managing Principal
John Pangrazio, Partner
Duncan Griffin, Designer
Fritz Johnson, Designer
Jin Ah Park, Designer
John Millard, Project Designer
Doug Keyes, Graphic Designer
Architect: ARC-NYC
Timothy Johnson, Principal
Model: Richard Tenguerian

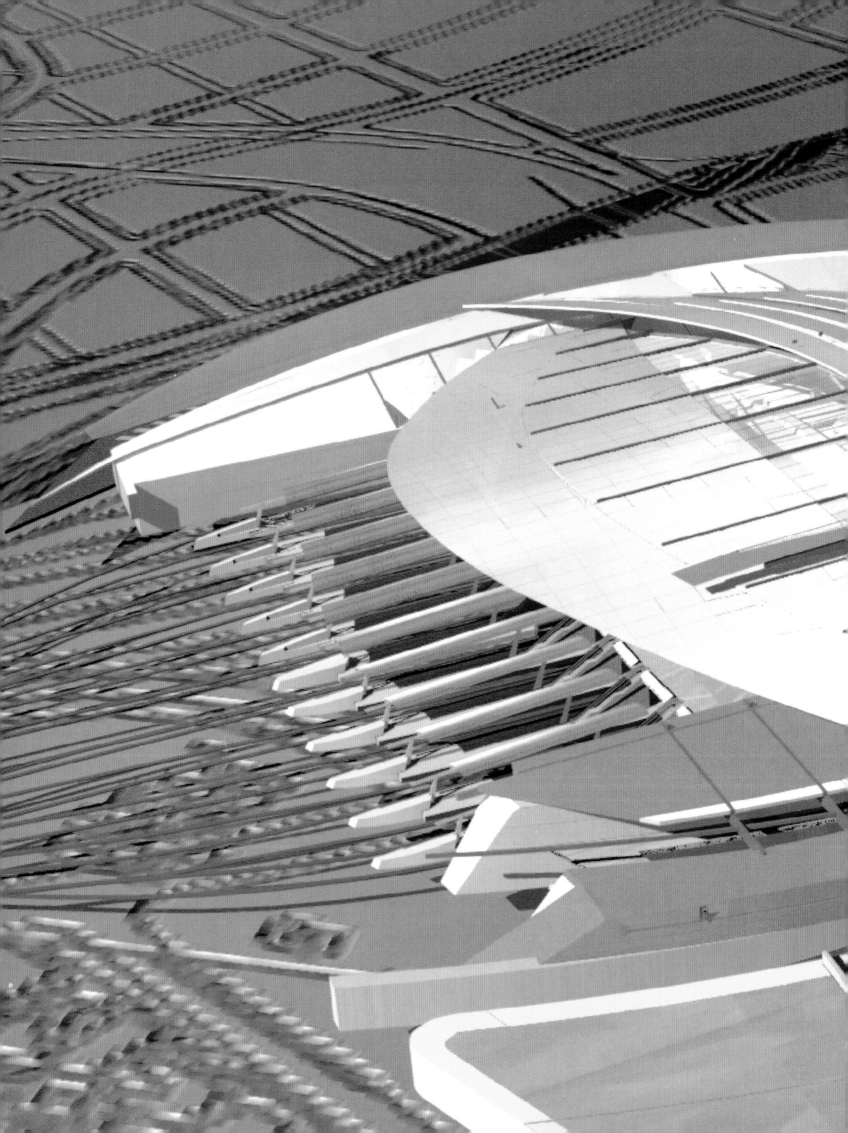

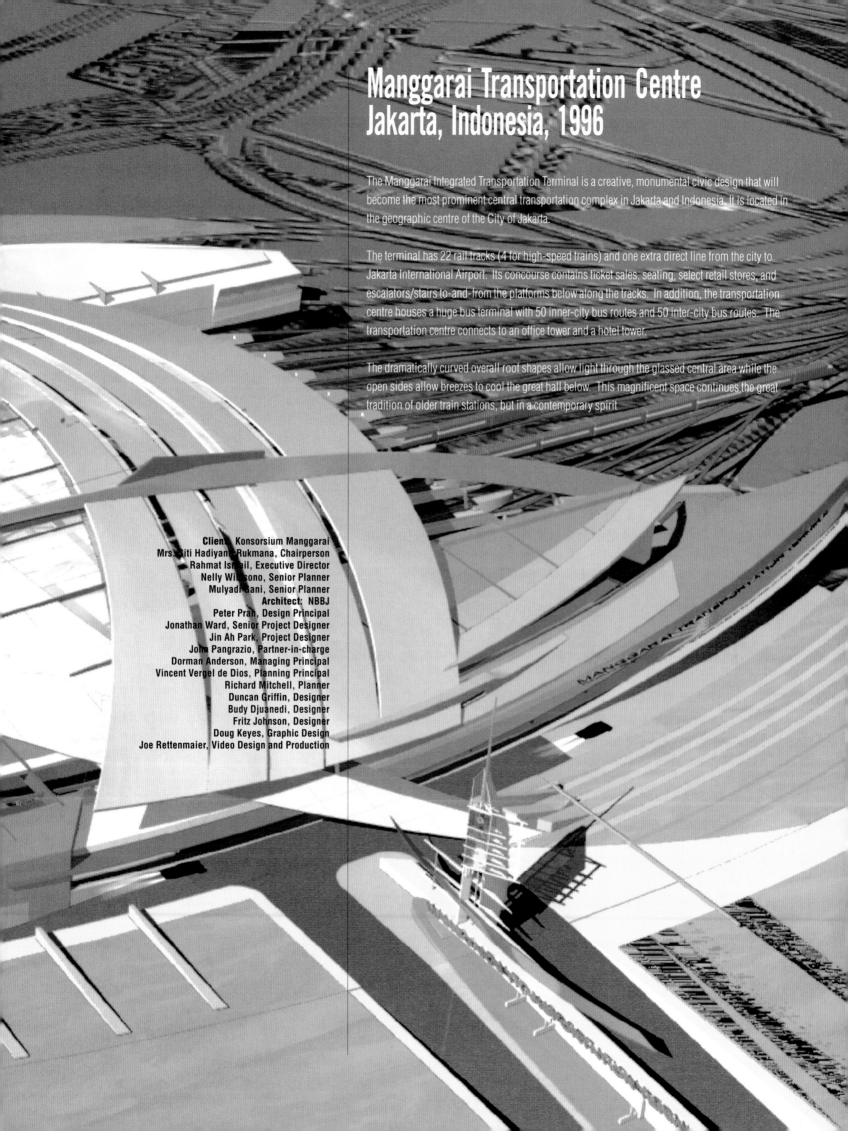

Manggarai Transportation Centre
Jakarta, Indonesia, 1996

The Manggarai Integrated Transportation Terminal is a creative, monumental civic design that will become the most prominent central transportation complex in Jakarta and Indonesia. It is located in the geographic centre of the City of Jakarta.

The terminal has 22 rail tracks (4 for high-speed trains) and one extra direct line from the city to Jakarta International Airport. Its concourse contains ticket sales, seating, select retail stores, and escalators/stairs to-and-from the platforms below along the tracks. In addition, the transportation centre houses a huge bus terminal with 50 inner-city bus routes and 50 inter-city bus routes. The transportation centre connects to an office tower and a hotel tower.

The dramatically curved overall roof shapes allow light through the glassed central area while the open sides allow breezes to cool the great hall below. This magnificent space continues the great tradition of older train stations, but in a contemporary spirit

Client: Konsorsium Manggarai
Mrs. Siti Hadiyanti Rukmana, Chairperson
Rahmat Ismail, Executive Director
Nelly Wibisono, Senior Planner
Mulyadi Bani, Senior Planner
Architect: NBBJ
Peter Pran, Design Principal
Jonathan Ward, Senior Project Designer
Jin Ah Park, Project Designer
John Pangrazio, Partner-in-charge
Dorman Anderson, Managing Principal
Vincent Vergel de Dios, Planning Principal
Richard Mitchell, Planner
Duncan Griffin, Designer
Budy Djuanedi, Designer
Fritz Johnson, Designer
Doug Keyes, Graphic Design
Joe Rettenmaier, Video Design and Production

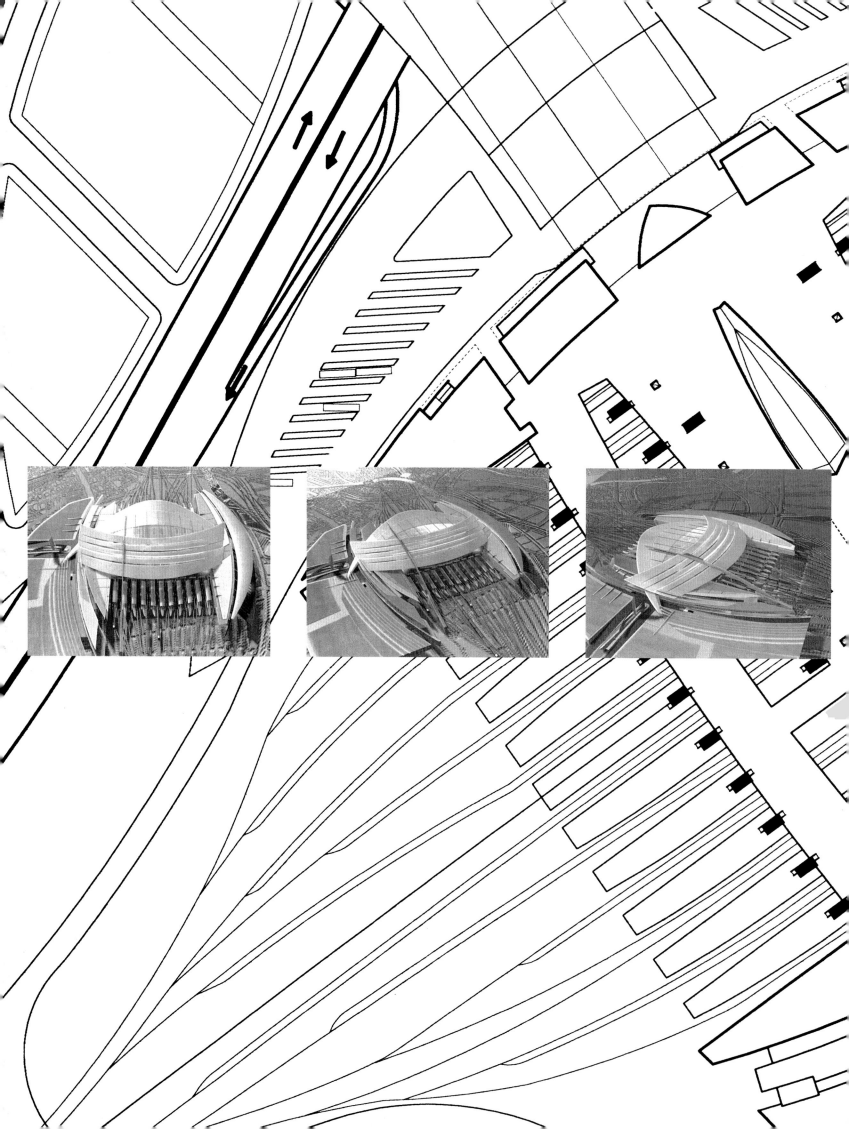

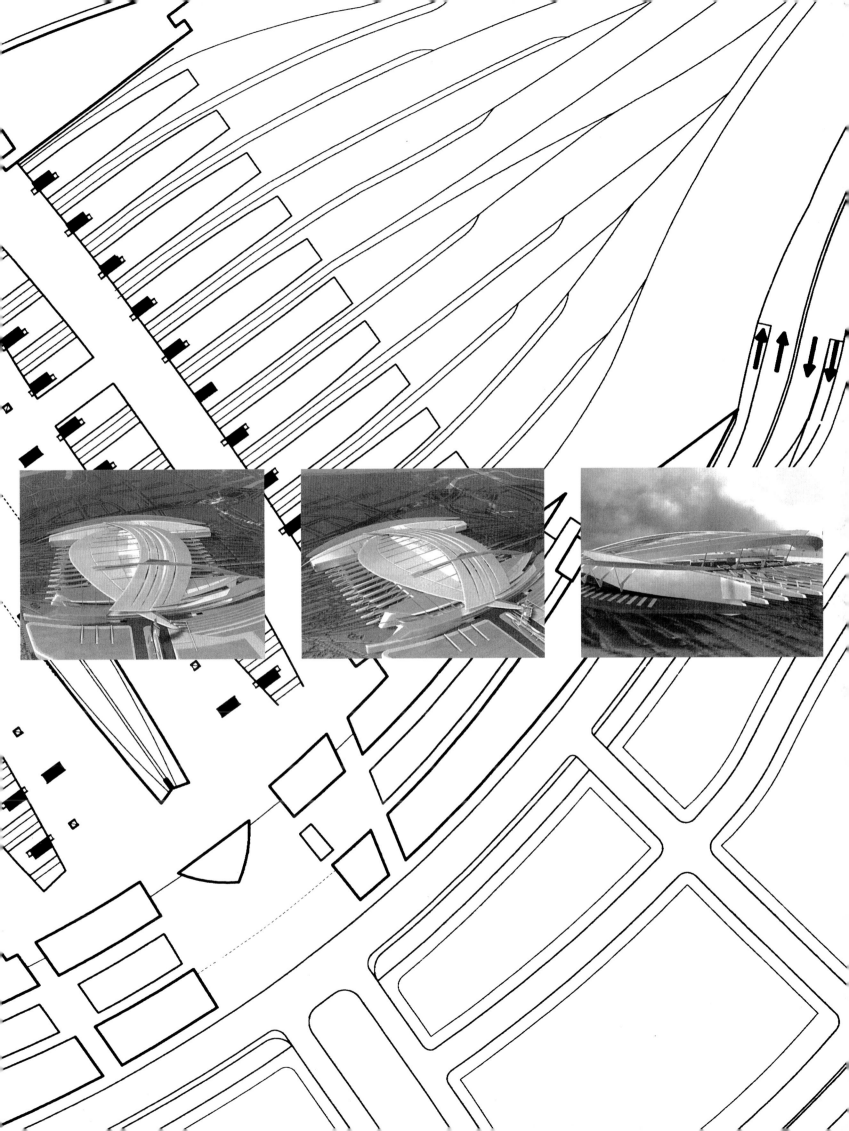

Section

El Presidente Apartment and Office Tower
Makati/Manila, Philippines, 1997

The architecture of El Presidente represents the future vision of the Philippines and of the client company, Duvaz. This mixed-use structure is situated on the main artery leading out of Makati, the central business district for the greater Manila region, towards Manila proper and Manila Bay. The effect is that Duvaz is formally positioning itself to move out of the traditional Philippines market and into international waters, while creating a gateway into and out of Makati.

The 60,000 sq.m programme calls for a 45-storey tower with a balanced ratio of office space in the lower half and residential above. The building is capped by a spectacular new office space for Duvaz, including a helipad and hangar, and maximum facilities for communications technology. The entire tower is lifted up on a 6-storey parking structure for 500 cars. Amenities in the basic programme include retail and restaurants on ground level, a health club and meeting facility on the deck between the tower and the parking podium, government commerce and trade offices on the two lower ground levels to provide support for tenants working to develop this international vision of the Philippines business community, and the latest in high-technology communications infrastructure.

The form, materials, and structure all express an overall vision of youth, movement and the future. The building takes on the form and identity of a glass sailing ship, defining the movement and exploration of Duvaz and the Philippines. The main gesture is a silver-blue glass sail on the north side of the building, curling and moving towards the bay. A sail on the water — or any form that propels itself through space — generally has a broad form which provides the lift through space, and a narrow face that slices through space. El Presidente also has this form. When looking at the sail from Makati, you see the narrow side moving away from the city; and from the water side you see a knife-blade cutting through the sky and moving towards the bay. From the other direction the sail is seen billowing in the sky. Its relationship to the other pieces is one of tension, keeping it taut in the wind.

The glass sail is placed and developed on the north side to take advantage of the low solar gain on that face. The concrete core, or mast, is placed on the south side of the building, effectively completing the passive solar strategy and shielding the building from the bulk of the solar gain. The side-loaded core also allows for the floor plate in this relatively tight site and small floor area to be free and flexible as well as allowing the tower to become very thin.

The parking structure is the engine that drives the tower. Formally the tower locks over it while the nose of the sail dips in front of it, cutting through space. It is clad in a series of folding screens, breaking free from the traditional, massive, block-like architecture of Makati. The double-stacked cars parked in this structure will become an economic engine for the project, helping finance the tower. Finally, the parking structure is a structural fulcrum pinning down the massive twisting of the very thin tower. El Presidente began excavation in late fall, 1997; full construction begins in winter, 1998.

Client: Duvaz Corporation
Judith Duavit-Vazquez, President and CEO
Burt Sinco, Project Architect
Architect Team: NBBJ/Lor Calma Associates
Architect: NBBJ
John Pangrazio, Partner
Peter Pran, Design Principal
Dorman Anderson, Managing Principal
Jonathan Ward, Senior Project Designer
Duncan Griffin, Project Architect
Budy Djuanedi, Project Manager
Jay Hallerin, Principal, Chief Cost Estimator
Carsten Stinn, Designer
Architect: Lor Calma Associates
Eduardo Calma, Design Principal
Donald Rivera, Senior Project Architect
Agnes Costiniano, Designer; Asa Almario, Designer
Structural Engineer: SWMB
Ron Klemencic, Principal in charge
Larry Karlson, Structural Design Manager
Ichiro Ikeda, Lead Structural Designer
Mechanical Engineer: Gregory Asia
Tony Cash, Creg Wilson
Construction Manager: Bechtel International
Max Muller, Project Director
Paul Majka, Design Manage

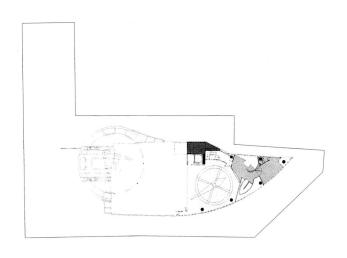

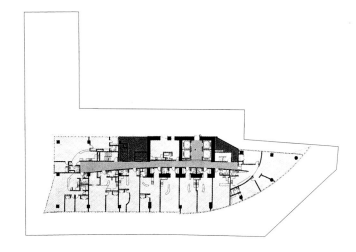

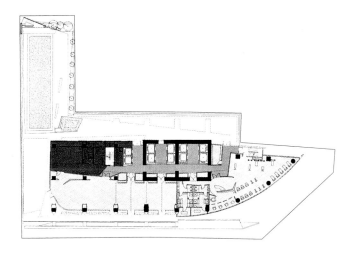

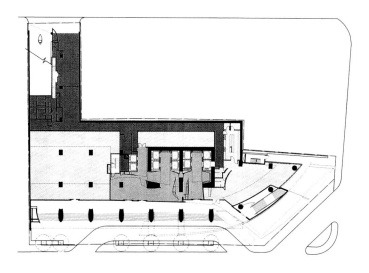

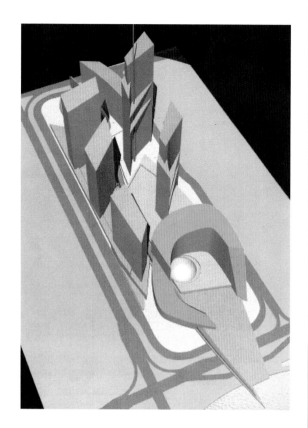

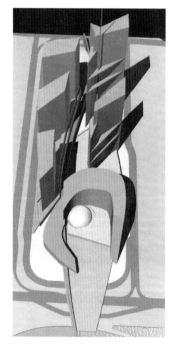

Stulang Commercial Development Johor, Malaysia, 1997

This master plan project consists of a major luxury hotel, four apartment buildings, a medical centre, and a performing arts centre. The site is located at the southern tip of Malaysia looking towards Singapore. It is located near the bridge to be built from Johor to Singapore.

The hotel has a bent overall shape, which defines the central exterior space within and at the same time provides magnificent views from all the hotel rooms; most of them face Singapore and the attractive waterfront. There is an exceptional energy in the overall master plan and in the movement of the different buildings, which are situated so that a maximum number of apartments have pleasant views and maximum light. The performing arts centre anchors the northern end of the site, while the hotel and its pedestrian pier to the south anchor it to the waterfront.

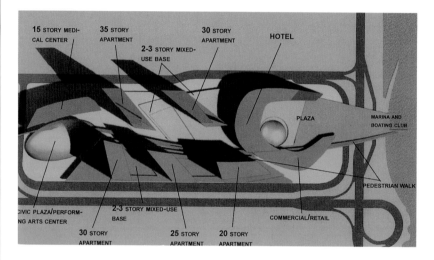

Client: TNB
Architect: NBBJ
John Pangrazio, Partner
Peter Pran, Design Principal
Jonathan Ward, Senior Project Designer
Dorman Anderson, Managing Principal
Architect in Kuala Lumpur: Focus Architects
Mohd Nazam Md Kassim, Director
Shah Sidek, Associate Director

Nihon TV Broadcasting Headquarters
Tokyo, Japan, 1997

Nihon Television Company owns a 15,000 sq.m site in Shiodome C-block, 1-chome, Higashi-Shinbashi, Minato-ku, Tokyo, for large scale urban development and its headquarters. The famous Ginza and Shimbashi areas are located just behind the Shiodome area, which forms an important traffic/transportation junction between Central Tokyo and the Bay area. To the southeast of the site is a water front housing the world's largest fish market, and adjacent to it is the Hamanikyu Garden. The plan includes a 50-storey headquarters tower, a lower, 35-storey hotel tower, broadcasting studios, an art gallery, banqueting floors, and a sunken plaza with retail shopping.

The Headquarters Tower and the Hotel Tower designs are site specific and reflect the urban design forces of heavy and light rail traffic patterns adjacent to the site. The elegant Headquarters design has an upward soaring quality that defies gravity and liberates the complex with views towards downtown Tokyo. The TV studios are within the lower podium levels which align with and feed off of the 50-storey core. They become the horizontal and vertical spine for NTV personnel. Tangential to the design forces of the Headquarters Tower and the Hotel Tower, the art museum is the centre of the complex and the heart of the sunken plaza that activates the lower floor levels of retail and is linked to adjacent sites to the north and east.

The design is an entry in an international invited architectural competition.

Architect Team: NBBJ/Ishimoto
Architect: NBBJ
Bill Bain, Partner
Peter Pran, Design Principal
Steve McConnell, Design Principal
Joey Myers, Senior Project Designer
Jim Jonassen, Consulting Partner
Architect: Ishimoto, Tokyo
Michio Sugawara, President & CEO
Shinsuke Kawahara, Director
Makoto Ishii, Director
Tsunagu Sato, Manager
Yasuhiro Kondo, Assistant Manager
Sano Koichiro, Chief - Structure
Ryuzo Tomita, Chief - Mechanical
Seiichi Nishikubo, Chief - Electrical
Hideto Takanaka, Architect/Competition Advisor

Client: US Airways
Philadelphia International Airport: Division of Aviation
Architects: NBBJ/Hillier
NBBJ
David Hoedemaker, Partner
Ted McCagg, Principal & Program Director
Peter Pran, Principal, Architecture - Lead Designer Principal
Alfred Moreno, Senior Project Architect/Manager
Joey Myers, Senior Project Designer
Joel McLeod, Senior Project Architect
Jonathan Ward, Designer
Jin Ah Park, Designer
Frederick Norman, Designer
Suzanne Zohr, Designer
Alec Vassiliadis, Model Designer
Gunther Winkelmann, Quality Assurance
Hillier
Steve DeRochi, Principal-in-charge
Dave McHenry, Program Manager
Scott Erdy, Senior Associate, Director of Design
Joe Augustine, Project Designer
Richard Ashworth, Project Architect
Jeffrey Mooney, Project Architect
Bruce Haxton, Project Administrator
Michael Levin, Project Architect
Bradley Lambertsen, Project Manager, Terminal One
Karl Pettit, Project Manager, Terminal A
Ian Taylor, Project Manager, Airside/Landside
Engineers: Ove Arup
Greg Hodkinson, Principal, Lead Engineer
John Burns, MEP
Dan Brodkin, Structural
Juan Alayo, Pedestrian/Vehicular Transportation
Peter Johnson, Fire Protection
Richard Ausser, Acoustics
URS Greiner
Paul Benefield, Baggage Handling
Oscar Martinez
Lynch Martinez, Retail Concessions
Pennoni Associates
Jonathan Esslinger, Traffic Engineering
Model Photography: Frederick Norman

Philadelphia International Airport
International Terminal
Philadelphia, Pennsylvania, 1998

The approved plan for International Terminal One has 23 gates, of which 19 are international gates and 4 are domestic gates. The total terminal gross area is 1,004,150 sq.ft. Levels One and Two define Departing, while Sterile Deplaning connections from the Second Level and the entire Third Level define Arrival — a unique arrangement that will work extremely well. (Most air terminals in the world have Arrivals on the lower levels and Departures on the upper levels.)

The flowing roof forms give the arrival hall extra height, ensuring that the act of arrival is a great experience. After arrival formalities and customs, passengers enter a light-filled open, lofty space with a view towards downtown Philadelphia.

The geometry of the concourses is at an angle to the terminal, requiring that the aircraft also move at an angle to the terminal thus giving a more dynamic impression than if the concourses were at right angles to it. This creates an exciting relationship between the concourse and the terminal building. The concept takes full advantage of this situation, evidenced by the sweeping movement from the new concourse into the terminal. When passengers move from the plane to the building, they will feel this movement as they deplane and pass through the facility.

The clear, strong circulation forms on the roof of the concourses tie them into the terminal, thus strengthening the overall composition. Other details of the existing concourse — including the apron lighting structures, the colour of the loading bridges (jetways) and the gate numbering — will be changed to improve quality within budget constraints, providing a unified composition.

Sea-Tac International Airport
Central Terminal
Seattle, Washington, 1998

This is the final opportunity for Sea-Tac International Airport to create an innovative, bold design statement that will become the gateway to Seattle and the Northwest; a new image that everyone will be proud of and an exhilarating, lively, pulsating retail space that most travellers would want to visit.

Seattle is the capital of aerospace, software, and biotech communication; it is a city set in a beautiful landscape; all of which should be expressed in an innovative modern design. Sea-Tac is a totally modern airport and so the new Central Terminal must be designed as modern architecture. Old train stations had arches and cupolas but such traditional forms have nothing to do with modern airport structures, which must look ahead of our time.

The design creates a bold, exuberant statement, which both embraces and ties in with the existing airport and with the new international terminal and hotel. The roof tapers up towards a crescendo at the centre, attracting people into its lofty, exciting, light-filled space, with shops, cafés, restaurants, waterfalls, exhibits, art works, and panoramic views.

Parallel to this overall design approach, retail, wayfinding, convenience and choice drive the interior design, which defines the solution from inside. This is an architecture of flight — elegant, embracing, comforting — with a magnificent interior performance space where the seating areas appear to float in space, as if poised on the wing.

Architect/Engineering Team: NBBJ/Weinstein-Copeland/Ove Arup
NBBJ Architects
David Hoedemaker, Partner
Ted McCagg, Principal and Director of Airport Facilities
Peter Pran, Design Principal
Joey Myers, Senior Project Designer
Alfred Moreno, Project Architect/Manager
Frederick Norman, Project Designer
Alec Vassiliadis, Model Designer
Joe Rettenmaier, Video Design
Roddy Grant, Graphic Design
Weinstein/Copeland Architects
Ed Weinstein, Partner
Julie A. Kriegh, Associate
Ove Arup Engineers
Peter Lassetter, Principal
Retail Consultant: Debbie DeGabrielle & Associates
Debbie DeGabrielle, Partner

Kwun Tong Town Centre
Hong Kong, 1998

Client: Land Development Corporation, Hong Kong
Abraham Razack, Chief Executive
Terry Arthur, Director, Planning Division
Roger M.H. Tang, Assistant Director, Planning Division
Architect: NBBJ
Jim Jonassen, Partner
Peter Pran, Design Principal
Dorman Anderson, Managing Principal
Jonathan Ward, Senior Project Designer
Joey Myers, Senior Project Designer
Duncan Griffin, Senior Project Architect
Hideto Tanaka, Project Designer (Ishimoto A&E, Tokyo, Japan)
Alec Vassiliades, Model Design
Susan Dewey, Graphic Project Manager
Paul Gillis, Graphic Design
Jordan Hukee, Graphic Design
Joe Rettenmaier, Video Design and Production
Structural Engineer: LERA
Les Robertson, Partner

The programme includes an 88-storey office tower and a 43-storey office tower, five residential towers — of which two are 65 stories, two are 43 stories, and one is 19 stories; and one is a 14-storey hotel with 145,000 sq.m. of retail. In addition, the lowest floor (at +5.00) is designated for the Bus Terminal. The MTR Station connects to the project; from the station there is a people-mover to bring people to the centre of the project, which is defined by a magnificent atrium. The total floor area for the project is 580,450 sq.m.

The site is located a few blocks away from the present Hong Kong International Airport; when the construction of the new Hong Kong International Airport is completed, the building heights for the Kwun Tong Town Centre will be acceptable. The site is defined by Mut Wah Street to the north west, Hip Wo Street to the east, and Kwun Tong Road to the south, with Tung Yan Street intersecting the site itself. There is a major North Gateway and a major South Gateway to the entire complex, with a secondary gateway from the west. A large, gently sloping Central People's Plaza opens up from the major North Gateway; this open plaza and green space is for the use of all the people living in the area, with special playgrounds for children and special areas for older people.

The town centre is seen as the heart of a city within the larger Hong Kong metropolitan area, a place where anything and everything can happen. The design of such a place should have an inherent spontaneity and power which makes it recognizable as a landmark.

The project is based on several key urban and architectural design goals coupled with an intuitive and emotional response to the site. There are many possibilities for linking the various programme elements into a place where people want to be, one that they will want to explore and experience. Inherent in the scheme is the juxtaposition of rational modern movement systems: buses, cars, and trains coexist with the gentle flow of pedestrian movement that shapes human places to live, shop, work and play.

The complex creates an identifiable landmark for Kwun Tong and for the future development of Kowloon. It provides clear pedestrian links from the existing MTR station to the bus terminals, and develops a clear, logical zoning of functions into a whole urban place; it allows for strong vertical zoning and the separation of vehicular and pedestrian traffic.

The development of the plaza, the town square, enables it to play the role of a centre for the project and for the Kwun Tong district as a whole. The outdoor plaza is complemented by an interior atrium where all the internal activities climax. It is a project of dignity and character and, simultaneously, it is a humane complex, a place that will be animated and full of life; a place where people will want to live and work and that they will visit.

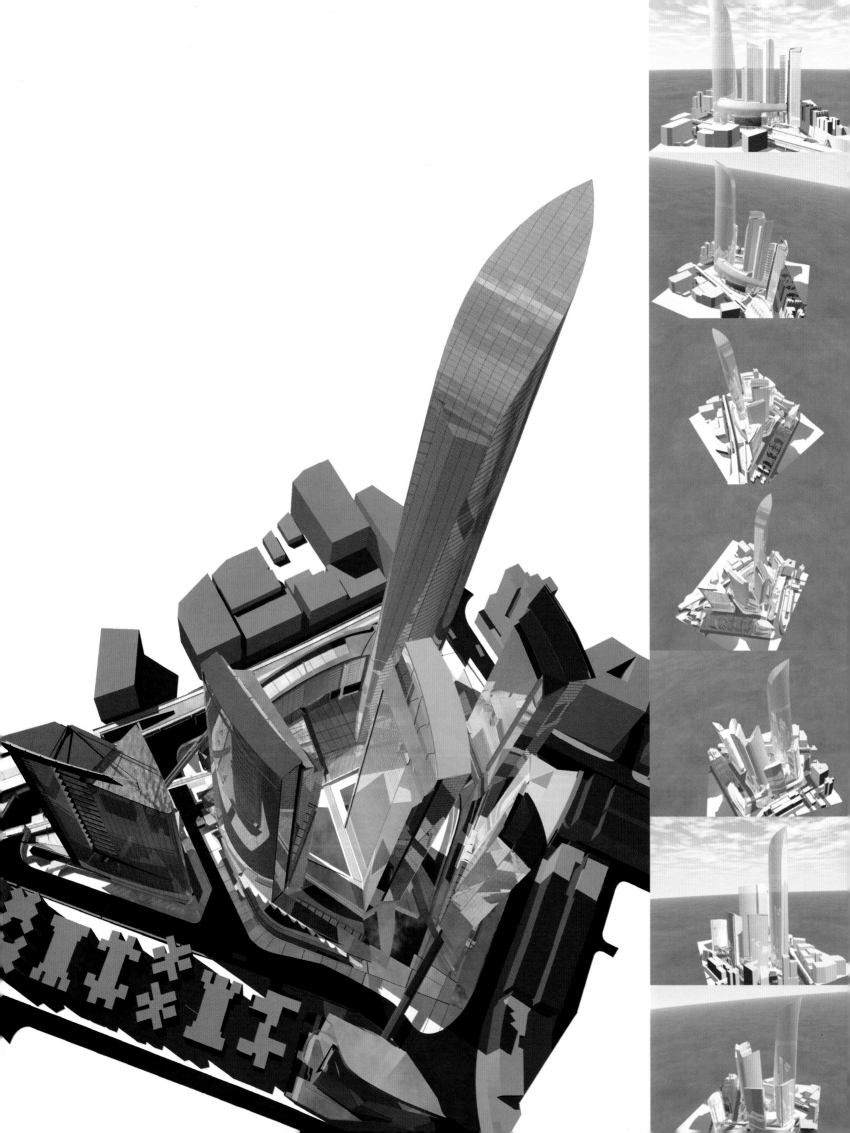

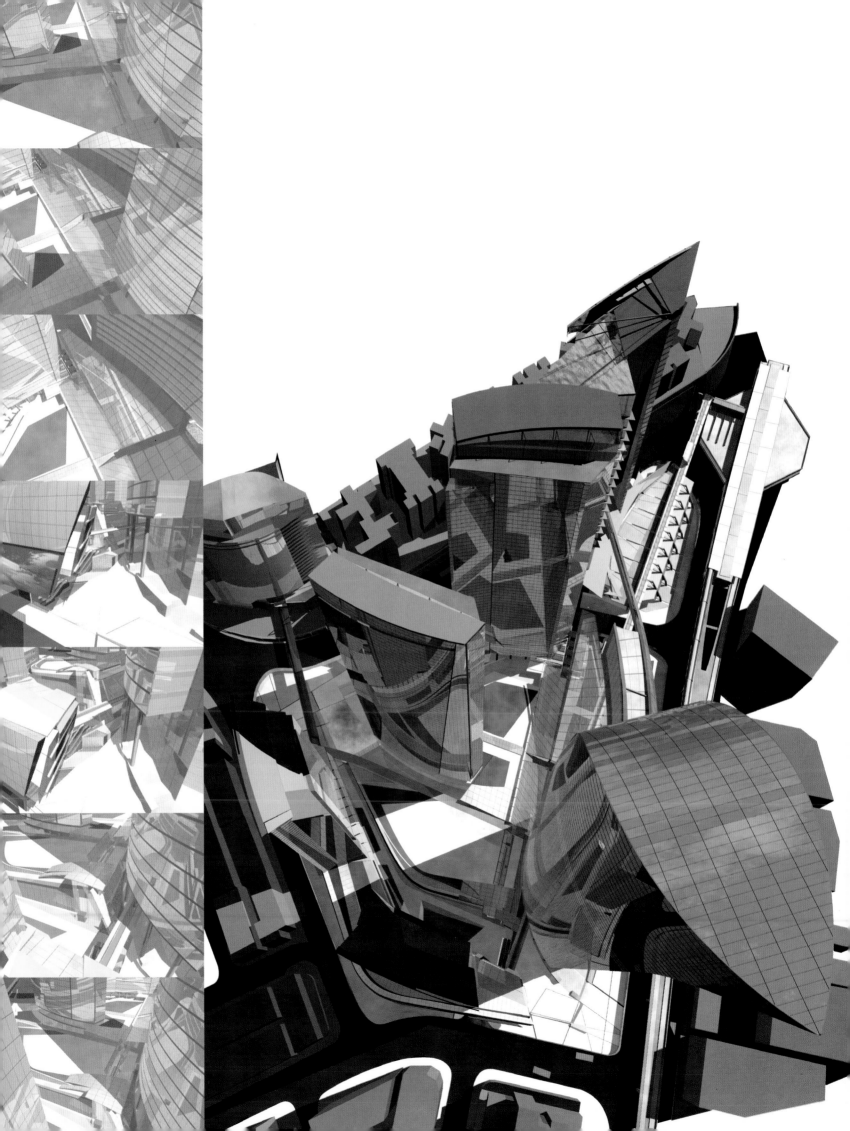

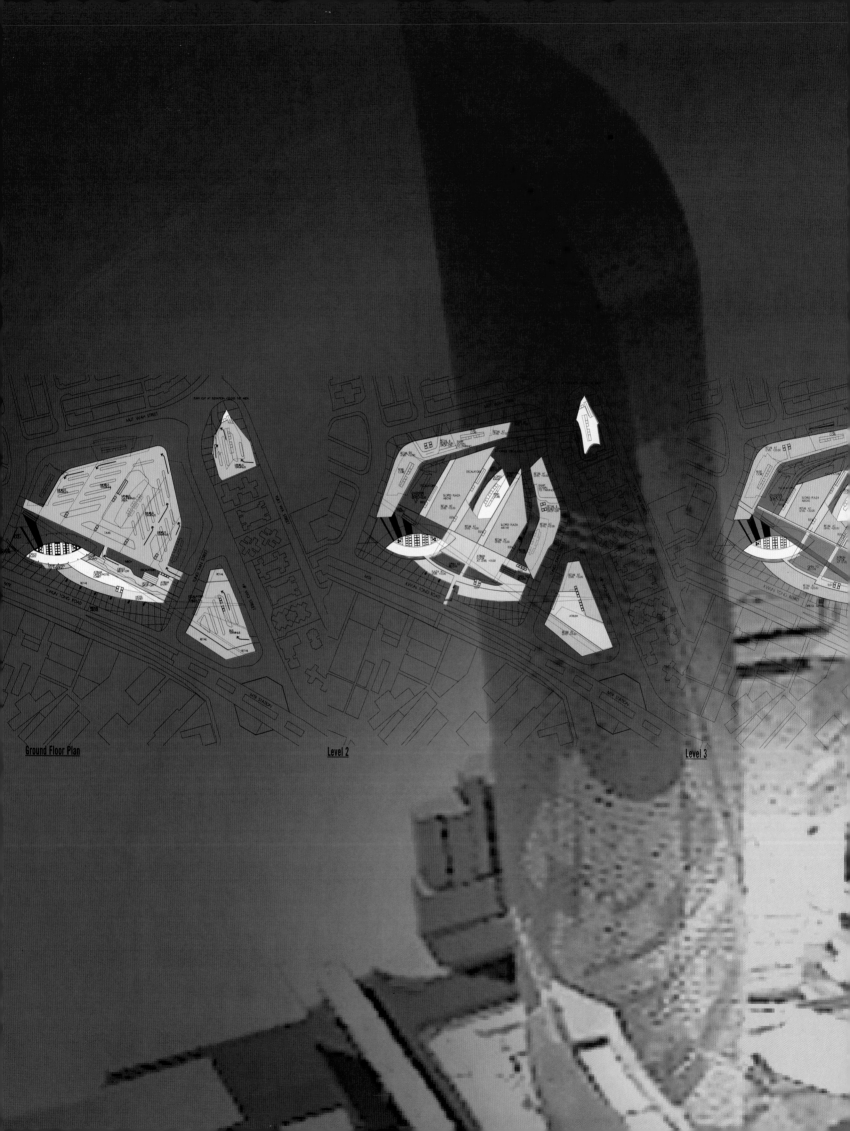

Ground Floor Plan

Level 2

Level 3

Level 4

Typical Level

This is the first prize and commission winner in the international competition for the new Telenor Headquarters to be built at Fornebu in Oslo, Norway, on the former site of Oslo International Airport. The competition was won in summer 1998 over six other finalists from Norway, Denmark, Sweden and England, including Richard Rogers+Snohetta, Niels Torp, and TTA+OKAW. When construction is complete in 2001-2002 this will be the largest office complex and building project in Scandinavia.

The building complex will be built on top of the main runway. The first phase of construction includes 136,000 sq.m of floor area; and the second phase will add another 64,000 sq.m, making a total floor area of 200,000 sq.m for the two phases. Six thousand Telenor staff will work there and so workplaces and meeting rooms are the dominant features of the complex. Fornebu is the most spectacular unbuilt site remaining in Oslo; it has a panoramic view of the Oslofjord, and is located only a ten-minute drive from downtown Oslo. The company requested an "office of the future" module with 30 persons per unit.

The chosen solution is located along the axis of the existing runway. Two curved circulation boulevards define the main entry, the central exterior plaza and their links to the main offices-of-the-future wings, as they move through and out of the complex towards the attractive Oslofjord. The main entry and the expo centre tie them together. Most of the work, meeting and circulation spaces have direct views of the waterfront and the Oslofjord; all have views of the surrounding countryside.

The main entry to the Headquarters building is open to the public and acts as a meeting place for Telenor's guests. The spacious arrival area is open, friendly and exciting, creating a focal point for the new city being developed at Fornebu. It is the heart of the headquarters building. Its auditorium, exhibition spaces, cafeterias, and expo centre are linked to the large glassed boulevards that are connecting links for the entire company.

The cultural centre at the eastern point of the complex is mostly for staff and invited guests but can be used by the general public for celebrations and special events. It has a number of spaces for various cultural activities, an art museum exhibit hall, library, theatre, dance rooms, party rooms, sports rooms, and workshops, for use during working and leisure hours.

The basic office units are connected horizontally in groups of from 2 to 6 units via bridges and recreational areas. This allows from 60 to 180 people to interact in each group. Vertically, the areas are connected via the atrium with its stairs and elevators. An average of 750 people can integrate in each block. The variation in the number of floors, the direction they face and the views they have ensures that each working area has its own special identity.

The boulevards permit variation, recreation, relaxation and chance meetings. The free, open forms are indicative of the company's democratic attitude to staff and their surroundings. The open east-west axis is an inviting gesture to those who come to Fornebu; it also provides views of the waterfront and free access to it. The remaining axis is a gesture to the former Fornebu — a celebration of the airport that brought so many people together in the twentieth century, a role that Telenor will play in the next century.

Telenor Headquarters
Fornebu, Oslo, Norway, 1998-

Site Plan

Client: Telenor
Telenor Fornebuproject Leadership:
Tom Henry Knudsen, Prosjektdirektör
Hedvig L. Hasund, Prosjektassistent
Ronald Sörgaard, Prosjektsjef
Arne Scott, Juridisk Sjef
Thormod Rogstad, Økonomidirektor
Mona Kolstad, Administrasjons- og Kvalitetssjef
Arve Paulsen, Informasjonsdirektör
Nina Dillingöen, Fagansvarlig Arkitekt
Marianne Vrangum, Prosjektkonsulent
Vigleif Naess, Prosjektleder
Einar Skjörten, Prosjektkoordinator
Aud Kevin, Prosjektsekretær
Knut Ramstad, Architect/Computer Expert
Åse Kleveland, Jury Chair for Architectural Design
Telenor Executives:
Thormod Hermansen, Konsernsjef/CEO
Magnus Dokset, Konserndirektör
Architects: NBBJ/HUS
NBBJ, USA
Scott Wyatt, Partner in charge
Peter Pran, Design Principal in charge of Design
Bill Nichols, Project Manager/Principal
Jim Waymire, Managing Principal
Joey Myers, Lead Senior Project Designer
Joe Herrin, Lead Senior Designer
Jonathan Ward, Lead Senior Designer
Jin Ah Park, Lead Senior Designer
Curtis Wagner, Lead Senior Designer
Mike Mora, Designer; Frederick Norman, Designer
Suzanne Zahr, Designer; Jeannine McAuliffe, Designer
Rysia Suchecka, Interior Design Advisor and Principal
Alec Vassiliadis, Model Design
Susan Dewey, Graphic Manager
Jordan Hukee, Graphic Designer
John Lodge, Model Design and Designer
Greg Lyons, Designer; Robert Anderson, Designer
Carsten Stinn, Designer
HUS, Norway
Björn Sörum, Partner in charge
Lars Christian Koren Hauge, Design Partner
Jan Störing, Senior Architect of Per Knutsen Architects
Hans Petter Mittet, Project Manager
Tom Forsberg, Lead Programme; Geir Bjordal, Programmer
Elisabeth Meyer, Architect; Torbjörn Caspersen, Architect
Nazare Lillebö, Architect;
Per Knudsen, Partner, PKA; Sven Erik Norholm, Partner, PTL
Model Photography: John Lodge, Maria Ryan Wagner

These pages and overleaf: 1st Phase

Concept Sketch, Level +20 and Level +16.5 Plans

This spread and overleaf: 2ND Fase

NBBJ Sports and Entertainment was selected after a rigorous international invited competition to design a multi-purpose, all-weather baseball stadium for the LG Group, in competition with Toyo Ito/Takanaka, Tokyo, Helmut Jahn, Chicago, and Nicholas Grimshaw/Ove Arup, London. The stadium is to be a symbol of Seoul which enters the 21st century as a city offering convenience, a new urban culture and space and opportunities for leisure. In addition, the stadium will be used for the 2002 World Cup Soccer Games.

The 43,000-seat Seoul Dome will provide a permanent home for the LG Twins baseball team and the ultimate corporate image for the LG Group. The programme includes the stadium, public concourse levels, cinemas, restaurants, an entertainment complex, an exhibition hall, a health club, banqueting facilities, department/retail stores, and a three-level parking garage.

The comprehensive concept for the project encompasses all functions in one design, and not in separate buildings for each of the main functions. This allows everyone who enters the complex to take part in a rich and diverse interweaving of functions, and to go from one activity to another — and then back again at any time using an electronic debit card. Under the dynamic roof with its highly articulated tectonic structure, a tube-like shape containing at one end the upper seating for a series of movie theaters is cantilevered over the main public entrance. There is a second tectonic arm of retail/entertainment, containing a 20,000 sq.m health club/spa, which bends towards the opposite corner of the site anchored by the ten-storey LG department store. The smooth tube-like structure and the tectonic bent machine structure become arms embracing the heart of the complex — the stadium. Both are full of movement and represent the duality of LG, which was created from two separate companies. The curved metal roof moves forcefully upwards (articulating a spirited sense of endlessness) towards the most active side of the site. Simultaneously, floating walkways move in the opposite direction. Tying the stadium and the entertainment functions together is a full-height, visually spectacular atrium, through which visitors continuously flow or linger.

The entire complex will be an important for the people of Seoul, the people of Korea, and for all those who visit it.

Seoul Dome
LG Twins Baseball Stadium/
2002 World Championship Football Stadium
+ Entertainment Centre,
Seoul, Korea, 1997-

Client: LG Group w/ Chang-Jo Architects
Architect: NBBJ Sports & Entertainment
Dan Meis, Design Principal
Peter Pran, Design Principal
Mike Hallmark, Principal in charge
Jim Jonassen, Partner
Jim Waymire, Managing Principal
Ron Turner, Principal
Ignatius Chau, Project manager
Jonathan Ward, Senior Project Designer
Joey Myers, Senior Project Designer
Michael Hootman, Senior Project Designer
Mike Amaya, Project Designer
Jonathan Emmett, Project Designer
Greg Lombardi, Project Designer
Brian Tessner, Designer
Peter Fergin, Designer
Greg Lyon, Designer
Salvador Hidalgo, Designer
Brent Whiting, Graphic Designer
Diane Anderson, Graphic Designer
Structural Engineers: SWMB
Jon Magnusson, Partner
Ron Klemencic, Principal in charge
Bryan Glover, Structural Designer
Paul Dietrick, Structural Designer
Model Photography: John Lodge

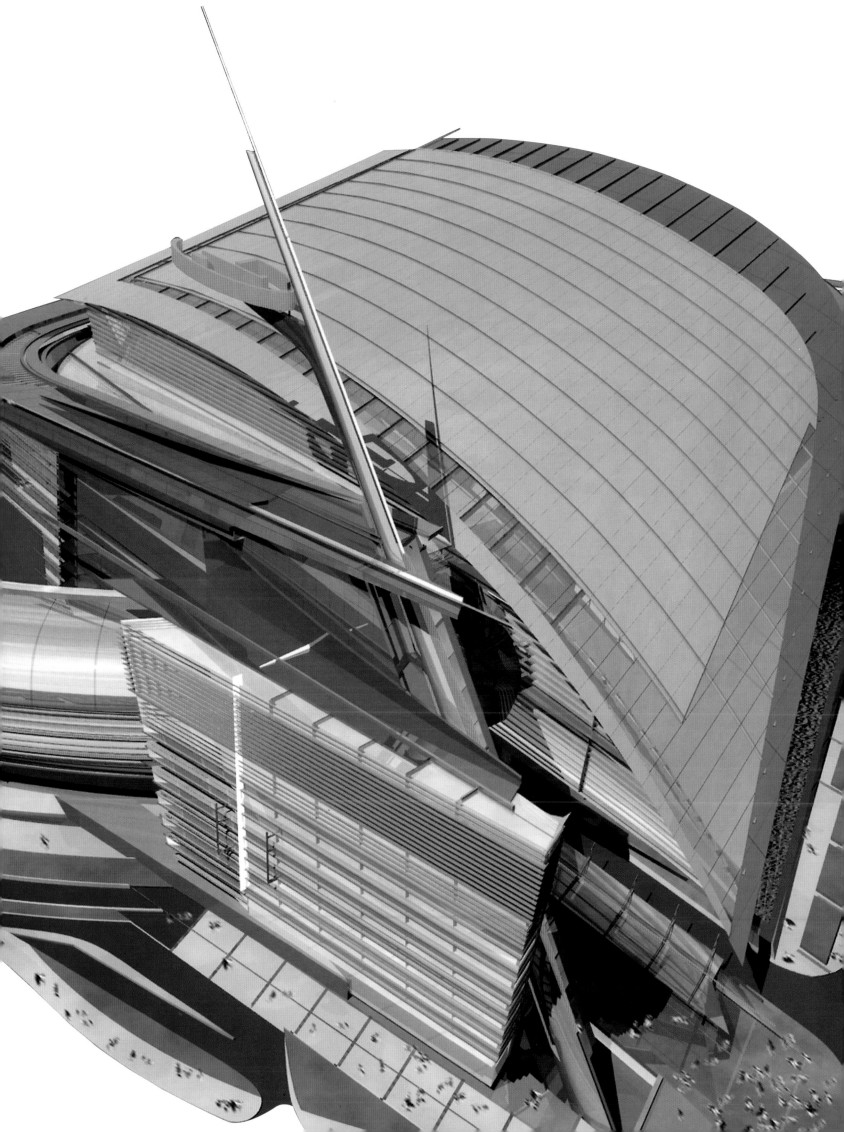

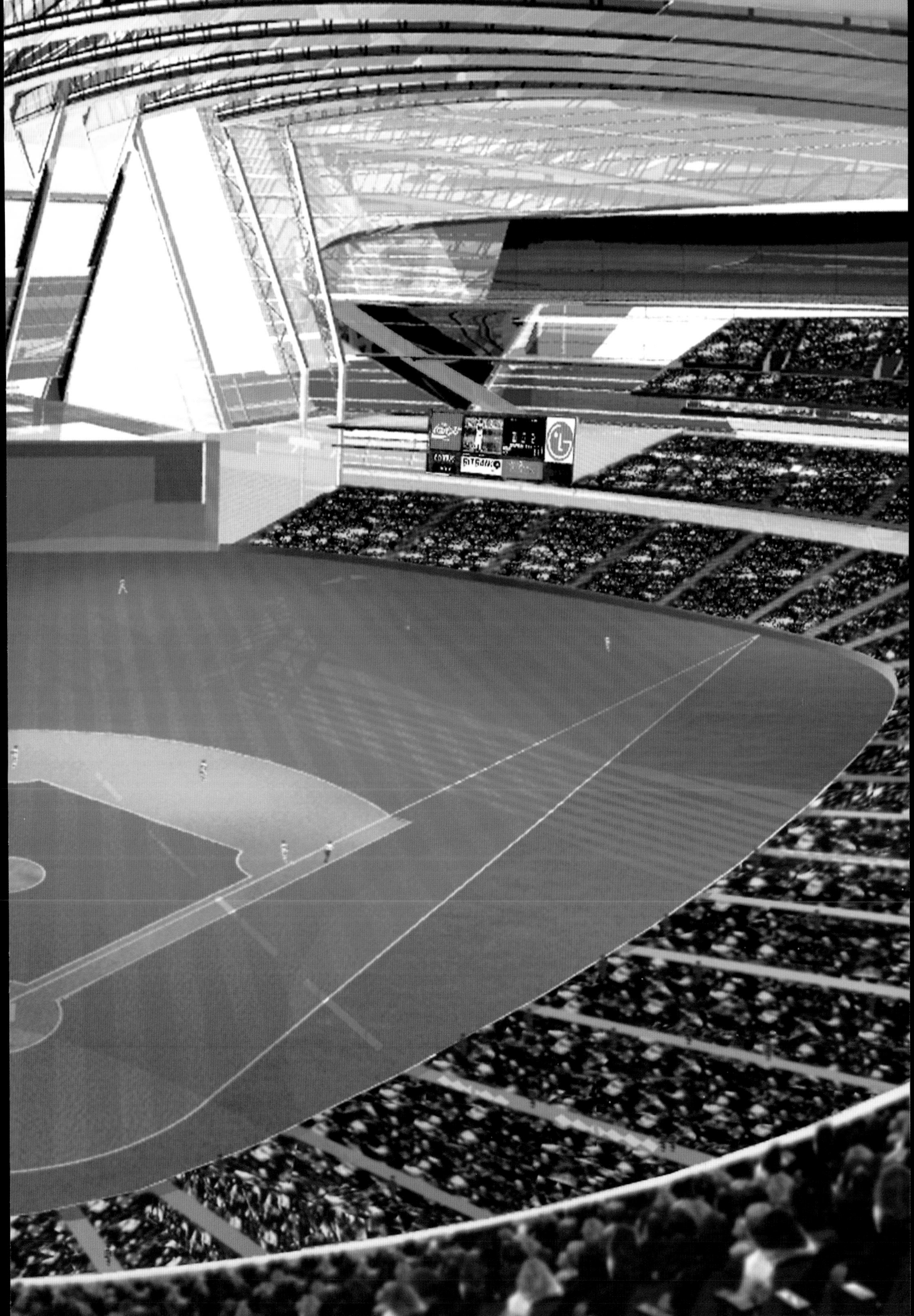

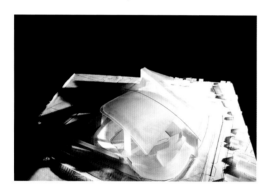
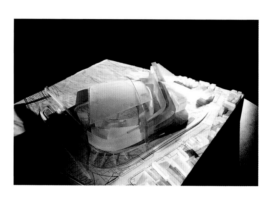
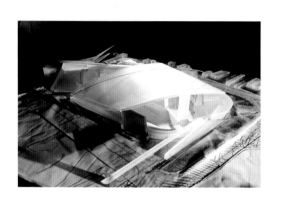

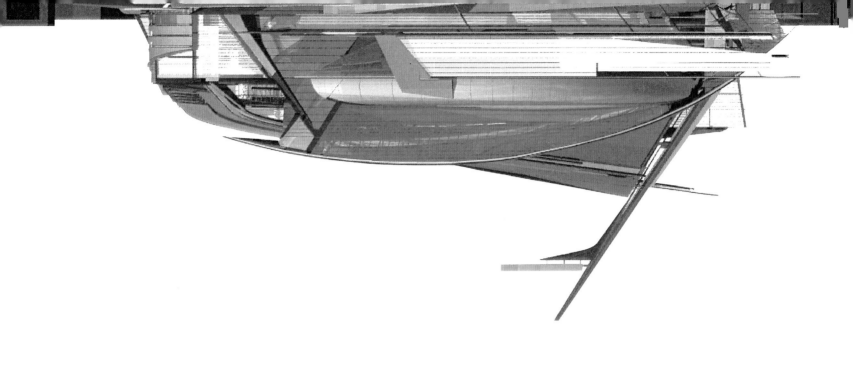

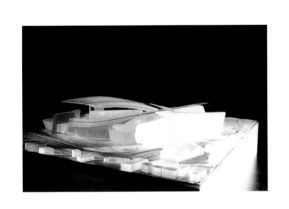
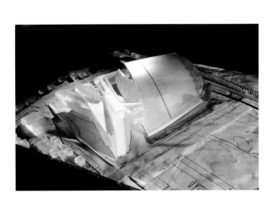
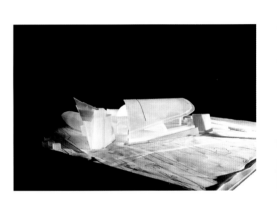

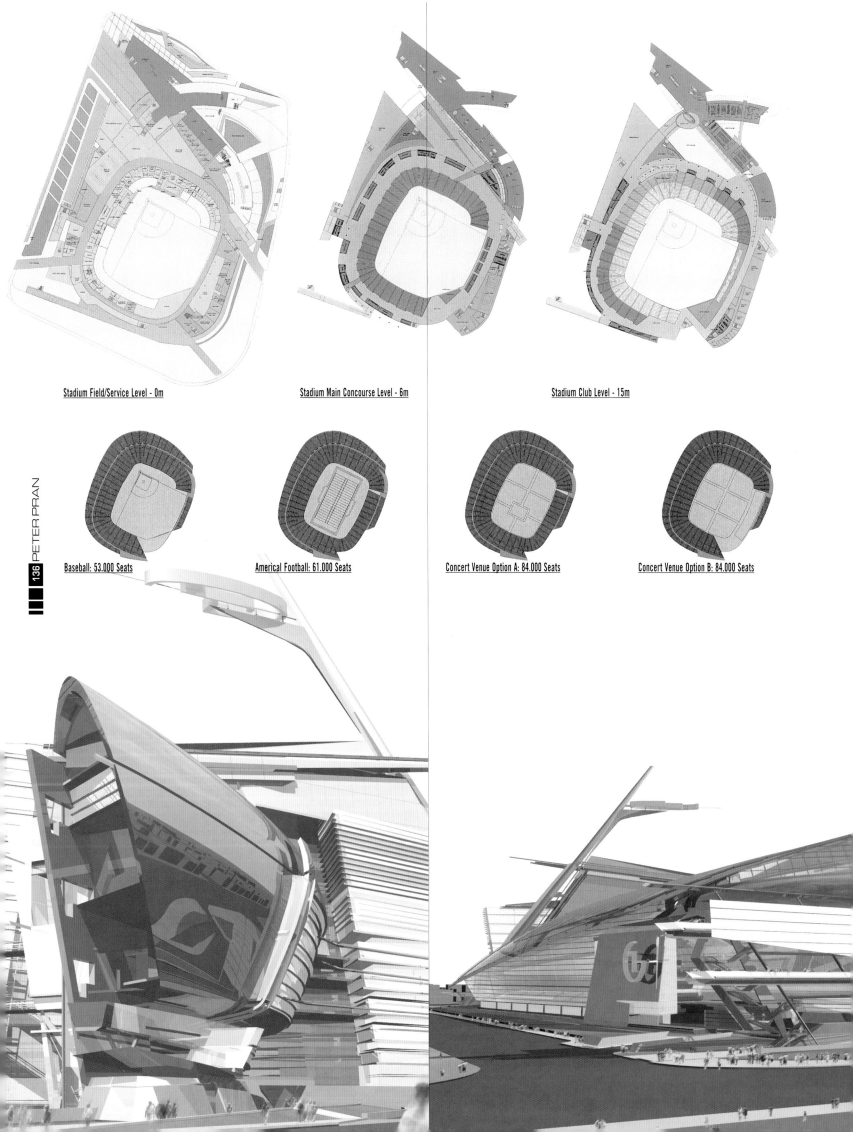

Stadium Field/Service Level - 0m

Stadium Main Concourse Level - 6m

Stadium Club Level - 15m

Baseball: 53.000 Seats

Americal Football: 61.000 Seats

Concert Venue Option A: 84.000 Seats

Concert Venue Option B: 84.000 Seats

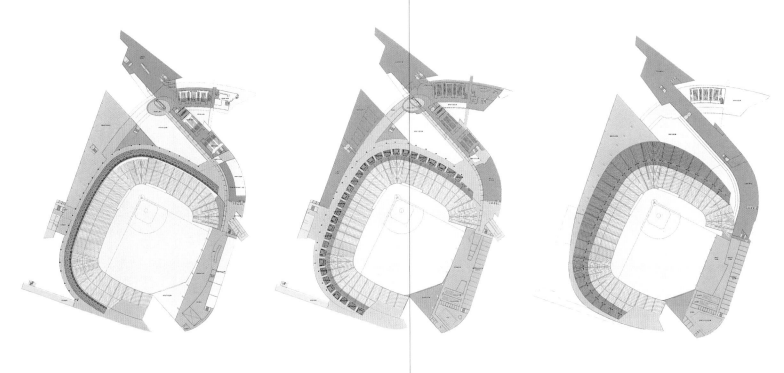

Stadium Suite Level - 18.5m   Stadium Upper Concourse Level - 23.9m   Stadium Upper Bowl - 35m

   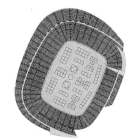   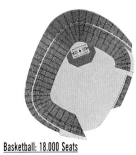

Soccer: 61.000 Seats   Exhibition Space: 84.000 Seats   Basketball: 18.000 Seats

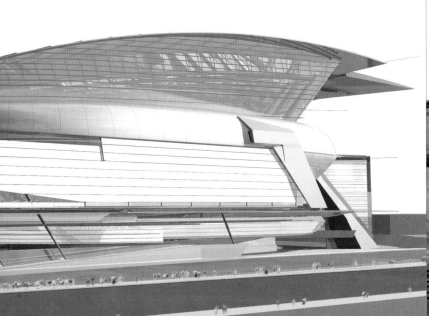

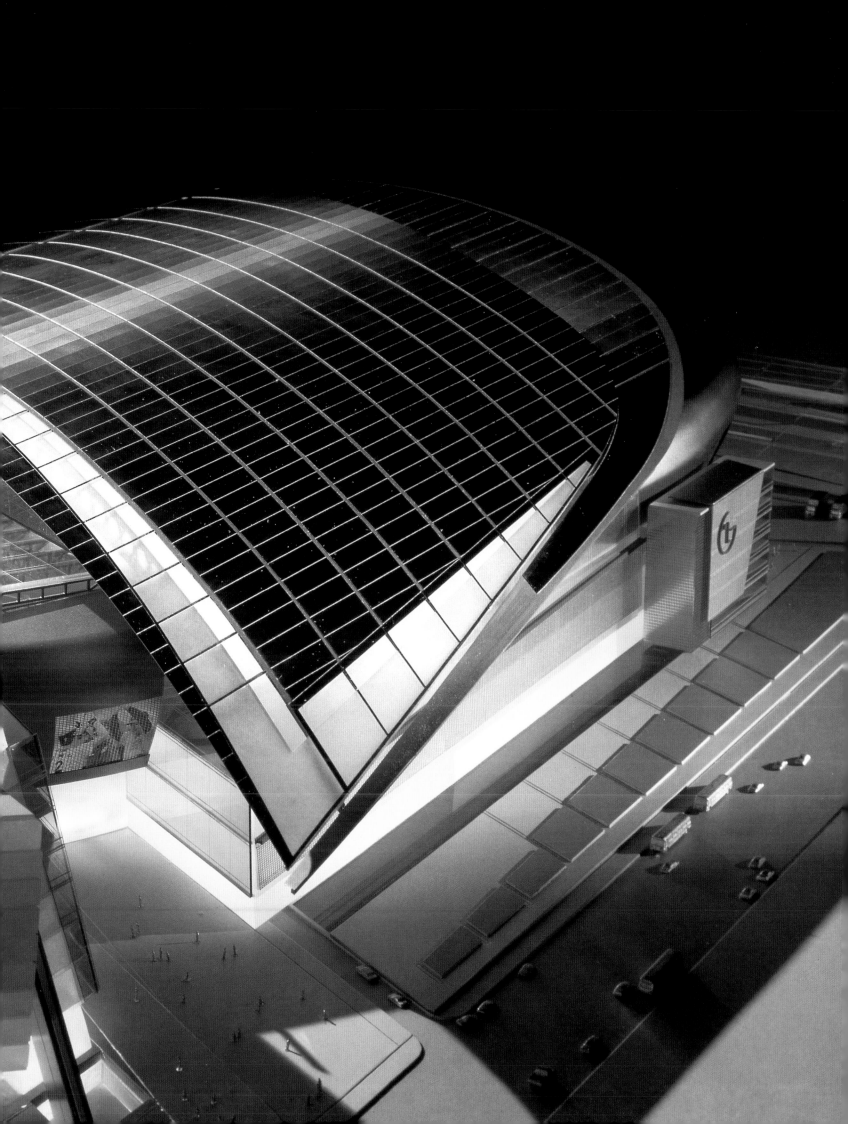

Peter Pran in Chicago

During Chicago's high-point of architectural development and construction in the 1960s and 1970s, Pran had the exceptional experience of working on several architectural masterworks.

Peter Pran worked with Mies van der Rohe for three years in his Chicago office as Project Designer on the National Gallery, Berlin, Germany; the Chicago Federal Center, Chicago, Illinois, USA; and the Toronto Dominion Center, Toronto, Ontario, Canada.

Peter Pran worked with SOM in Chicago for seven years. During that time he was Project Designer on the Jeddah International Airport, Jeddah, Saudi Arabia, and on the CTA Rapid Transit Stations, Chicago, Illinois, USA, both in collaboration with Myron Goldsmith, Design Partner, and with Fazlur Khan, Structural Partner. He was invited in by Fazlur Khan to work on architectural/structural concept models and studies with the design team in the schematic phase (only) on the Sears Tower, Chicago, Illinois, USA; Bruce Graham was Design Partner in charge and Fazlur Khan the Structural Partner in charge of the Sears Tower.

On Peter Pran's Master of Architecture that he received from Illinois Institute of Technology, Chicago, Myron Goldsmith, Fazlur Khan, as well as David Sharpe, were his advisors; his thesis included a large Convention Hall for Chicago.

Peter Pran co-authored the book *100 Years of Architecture in Chicago*, with Franz Schultze and Oswald Grube, and co-authored the exhibit at the Museum of Contemporary Art in Chicago; he received the AIA Illinois Honor Award for both accomplishments.

Biographies

PETER PRAN

Born in Oslo, Norway

Education
Master of Science in Architecture, Illinois Institute of Technology, Chicago, Illinois, 1969
Bachelor of Architecture/Diploma Architect, Oslo Arkitekthögskole University, Oslo, Norway, 1961

Professional Positions
Design Principal, NBBJ, Seattle (and Los Angeles), USA
Design Principal and Senior Vice President, Ellerbe Becket, New York, USA (10 years)
Director of Design and Associate Partner, The Grad Partnership, Newark, New Jersey, USA (2 years)
Director of Design and Associate, Schmidt, Garden & Erikson, Chicago, USA (6 years)
Senior Architect/Senior Designer, Skidmore, Owings & Merrill, Chicago, USA (7 years)
Architect and Project Designer, Mies van der Rohe, FAIA, Chicago, USA (3 years)
Architect/Project Designer, Nils Holter, Oslo, Norway (2 years)

Academic Positions
Distinguished Rose Morgan Visiting Professor of Architecture, University of Kansas, USA
Visiting Professor, Faculty of Architecture, University of Washington, Seattle, Washington, USA
Visiting Professor, Royal Danish Academy of Fine Arts, School of Architecture, Copenhagen, Denmark
Visiting Professor of Architecture, Kanto Gakuin University, Yokohama/Tokyo, Japan
Distinguished Adjunct Professor of Architecture, New York Institute of Technology, Old Westbury, New York, USA, (6 years)
Visiting Professor of Architecture, University of Palermo, Palermo, Italy
Adjunct Associate Professor of Architecture, New Jersey Institute of Technology, Newark, New Jersey (4 years)
Visiting Associate Professor of Architecture, University of Illinois, Urbana-Champaign, Illinois (1 year)
Adjunct Associate Professor of Architecture, University of Illinois, Chicago (8 years)
Assistant Professor of Architecture, Washington State University, Pullman, Washington (4 years)

Registration
Registered Architect: New York, Michigan, Washington, Wisconsin
Licensed Architect: Norway, Sweden, Denmark

Professional Organizations/Affiliations
American Institute of Architects (National): AIA Member
New York Chapter, American Institute of Architects
Seattle Chapter, American Institute of Architects
Norwegian Architects' Association: MNAL member
Who's Who in America, 1986-1998

Design Prizes
First Prizes in the following national/international architecture competitions:
Telenor Headquarters, Fornebu, Oslo, Norway. First prize and commission, competing with Richard Rogers, England + Snohetta, Norway; Neils Torp, Norway; Telje-Torp-Aasen/OKAN, Norway; Vandkanten, Denmark; Nielsen, Nielsen, Nielsen, Denmark and a joint team from Sweden.
Seoul Dome 21, 2002 World Championship Football Stadium and Baseball Stadium + Sports and Entertainment Center with theatres, exhibition centre, and retail, Seoul, Korea. International architecture competition, competing with Toyo Ito/Takanaka, Tokyo; Nicholas Grimshaw/Ove Arup, London; and Helmut Jahn, Chicago, 1997. Winning NBBJ design team: Peter Pran, Dan Meis, Michael Hallmark, Jonathan Ward, Joey Myers, Jim Jonassen, Jim Waymire, Jonathan Emmett, Michael Hootman, Mike Amaya
Asian Center, 70-storey plus 50-storey plus commercial centre for Daewoo, 1997, with NBBJ
Sea-Tac Office Complex; Seattle, Washington, 1997, with NBBJ
80-storey Jakarta Mixed-use Tower; Jakarta, Indonesia, 1996, with NBBJ
Dayton Commercial & Cultural Center; Dayton, Ohio, USA, 1996; with NBBJ

Karet Office Tower (40-storey); Jakarta, Indonesia, 1995
Tip Top Tailors Master Plan; Toronto, Ontario, Canada, 1994
New York Police Academy; New York, New York. 1992-93 (in competition with Sir Norman Foster, England; Robert Venturi, USA; Rafael Viñoly, USA; and Larabee Barnes, USA)
Bin Laden/Samarec Headquarters; Jeddah, Saudi Arabia, 1992
New Chicago Stadium & McCormick Expansion; Chicago, Illinois, 1991
New York Psychiatric Institute; New York, New York, 1991
Canadian National/Royal Trust Office high-rise; Ontario, Canada, 1990
Rikshospital; Oslo, Norway, 1990
Newspaper Headquarters; Oslo, Norway, 1989

Design Awards
National/American Institute of Architects Interior Design Award
Two *Progressive Architecture* National Design Awards
AIA National Design Award & National Modern Health Care Design Award
New York City and State/American Institute of Architects Design Awards: 12 Design Awards
American Collegiate Schools of Architecture: National Design Award
Chicago and Illinois/American Institute of Architects Design Awards: 2 Design Awards
Kansas City/AIA Design Award
Service Award for co-authoring book on "*100 Years of Chicago Architecture*," 1976, from Illinois AIA.
Book authored by Franz Schulze, Peter Pran, and Oswald Grube

Other Specific Awards and Honours
1995 AIA National Design Award and Health Care Award, New York State Psychiatric Institute
1992 National AIA Interior Design Award of Excellence, 1992, and Interior Design Award, New York Chapter, American Institute of Architects, 1990, for Deloitte & Touche Headquarters, Wilton, Connecticut
1991 New York Chapter, American Institute of Architects Design Award, 1990 and *Progressive Architecture* Design Award 1991, for CN/Royal Trust Office Complex, Toronto
1991 Design Award, New York Chapter, American Institute of Architects, for Banco Popular, Quito, Ecuador
1991 Design Award, New York Chapter, American Institute of Architects, for New Rikshospital, Oslo
1989 The NYC/AIA Design Jury gave three 'Special Awards for Body of Work' to Richard Meier (for three projects); to Peter Eisenman (for three projects); and to Peter Pran, Design Principal (for three projects)
1989-90 National Design Award from American Collegiate Schools of Architecture, 1990 and New York Chapter, American Institute of Architects Design Award, 1989, for Consolidated Terminal for American Airlines/Northwest Airlines, John F. Kennedy International Airport, New York
1988 Design Award, New York Chapter/American Institute of Architects, for New Hartford City Hall, Hartford, Connecticut
1988 Honorary Citizen of Minnesota (appointed by Governor Perpich)
1988-89 *Progressive Architecture* Design Award 1989, and New York Chapter/American Institute of Architects Design Award, 1989 for Schibsted-Ditten Project, Headquarters for *Aftenposten* and *Verdens Gang* newspapers, Oslo, 1989
1987 Design Honour Award, New York Chapter, American Institute of Architects, for South Ferry Plaza, New York
1986 Design Honour Award from New York Chapter/American Institute of Architects, for Entry and Lobby, 233 Park Avenue South, New York
1984 National Design Award, Passaic County Juvenile Detention Facility, Haledon, New Jersey, from National AIA and ACA
1983 Second Prize in National Design Competition, Codex Corporation Headquarters, Mansfield, Massachusetts
1982 Design Award for Recreation Building, Marian College, Wisconsin, from Chicago Architectural Club
1981 Award Mention for Facilities Center, Indianapolis, from Chicago Architectural Club
1981 Second Prize in Architectural Competition for Pittsburgh Center for the Arts Addition, Pittsburgh, Pennsylvania
1980 National Design Awards, from *Architectural Record*, UCLA, Columbia University and AIA Health Care Program for Family Health Center, Gary, Indiana and for Petersburg Psychiatric Institute, Petersburg, Virginia.
1978 First Prize in Chicago Townhouse Competition, sponsored by

Graham Foundation
1977 Outstanding New Citizen Award, from Citizenship Council of Metropolitan Chicago
1977 Distinguished Building Design Award, Chicago Chapter AIA, and Building Design Honour Award, Illinois Council AIA, for Museum in Chicago
1976 Illinois State AIA Service Award, for co-authoring book *100 Years of Architecture in Chicago: Continuity of Structure and Form*, and co-organizing exhibit on same subject at the Museum of Contemporary Art in Chicago.

Selected Buildings and Projects
1998 New York State Psychiatric Institute, Manhattan, New York City, NY, USA - built
1998 New Academic Buildings, State University of New York at Binghamton, New York, USA - built
1998 Telenor Headquarters, Oslo, Norway - to be built
1998 Seoul Dome 21 Sports and Entertainment Centre, Seoul, Korea - to be built in 1999)
1998 Philadelphia International Airport; International Terminal, Philadelphia, PA, USA
1998 Sea-Tac International Airport, Central Terminal, Seattle, Washington, USA
1998 Graha Kuningan 50-storey Office Tower, Jakarta, Indonesia (under construction)
1998 Kwun Tong Town Centre, Hong Kong (planned to be built)
1998 El Presidente, Apartment and Office Tower, Manila, Philippines (to be built in 1998)
1998 Karet Office Tower, 40-storey Office Tower, Jakarta, Indonesia (to be built in 1998)
1997 New Jakarta City Centre and Manggarai Transportation Centre, Jakarta, Indonesia (to be built)
1997 PSP 40-storey Apartment Towers, Jakarta, (to be built)
1997 Stulang Mixed-use Development, Johor, Malaysia
1997 Sea-Tac Office Complex, Seattle, Washington, USA
1997 Nihon TV Broadcasting Centre, Tokyo, Japan
1996 Curitiba Arena-Hotel-Retail, Curitiba, Brazil
1996 Dayton Cultural and Commercial Center, Dayton, Ohio, USA
1996 PMR Executive Interiors Menara-Imperium, Jakarta, Indonesia - built
1996 80-storey Mixed-use Tower, Jakarta, Indonesia
1995 Seoul Broadcasting Centre, Seoul, Korea
1995 California State Office Building, Oakland, California, USA
1995 Flamengo Football Stadium, Rio de Janeiro, Brazil
1995 TNB Headquarters Tower, 60-storey, Kuala Lumpur, Malaysia
1994 Boston Gardens Arena, Boston, Massachusetts, USA - built
1994 Kiel Arena, St. Louis, Missouri, USA - built
1994 Portofino Diamond C 40-storey Apartment Tower, Miami, Florida, USA
1994 Tip Top Tailor Building, Toronto, Canada
1993 New York Police Academy, The Bronx, New York City, NY, USA
1992 Staten Island Development Center, Staten Island, New York, USA - built
1992 Bin Laden/Samarec Corporate Headquarters, Jeddah, Saudi Arabia
1992 New Entry, Kings Hill Development, Kent, England
1992 De Centrale in Den Haag, The Hague, The Netherlands
1991 Banco Popular, Quito and Ibarra, Ecuador
1991 Resort Hotel, Okinawa, Japan
1991 New Rikshospital, Oslo, Norway
1991 Columbia University, Research Centre for Disease Prevention, New York City, NY, USA
1990 Deloitte & Touche Headquarters, Wilton, Connecticut, USA - built
1990 Canadian National/Royal Trust Development, Toronto, Canada
1990 CN/Labatts headquarters, TV Studios, Toronto, Canada
1990 New Chicago Stadium and McCormick Place Addition, Chicago, Illinois, USA
1989 Headquarters for Schibsted Gruppen newspapers *Aftenposten* and *Verdens Gang*, Oslo, Norway
1989 New Consolidated Terminal for American Airlines/Northwest Airlines, JFK International Airport, New York City, NY, USA
1987 South Ferry Plaza, New York City, NY, USA
1987 New Hartford City Hall, Hartford, Connecticut, USA
1986 233 Park Avenue South, New York City, NY, USA - built
1984 Prudential Short Hills Office Complex, Short Hills, New Jersey, USA
1983 Codex Headquarters, Mansfield, Massachusetts, USA

1982 Facilities Centre, Indianapolis, Indiana, USA - built
1980 Family Health Centre, Gary, Indiana, USA - built
1979 Emergency Wing, Methodist Hospital, Gary, Indiana, USA - built
1979 Recreation Centre, Marian College, Fond du Lac, Wisconsin, USA - built
1976 Jeddah International Airport, Jeddah, Saudi Arabia - built
1976 Diamond Shamrock Headquarters, Concord Township, Ohio, USA - built
1973 Khaneh Centre, Tehran - partially built
1972 KRPL Radio & Television Station and Offices, Moscow, Idaho, USA - built
1969 Sears Tower, Chicago (schematic design only, in collaboration with Fazlur Khan) - built
1968 CTA Rapid Transit Stations, Chicago, Illinois, USA - built
1966 Toronto Dominion Centre, Toronto, Ontario, Canada (with Mies van der Rohe) - built
1965 Chicago Federal Center, Chicago, Illinois, USA (*with Mies van der Rohe) - built
1963 National Gallery, Berlin, Germany (with Mies van der Rohe) - built
1962 New National TV Building, Oslo, Norway - built

Publications

Recent Feature Articles:

L'ARCA, "Seoul Dome: 2002 World Championship Football Stadium/Baseball Stadium and Entertainment Center," by Peter Pran, Dan Meis, Michael Hallmark, Jim Jonassen, Jonathan Ward, Joey Myers, Jim Waymire, Jonathan Emmel, Michael Hootman, Mike Amaya of NBBJ Los Angeles and Seattle, in January 1998 issue (including cover).

NEW ARCHITECTURE, International architecture magazine, London, England. Article on "Peter Pran's Recent International Tower Projects" No. 1, 1997. Towers co-designed with Jonathan Ward and Timothy Johnson.

LA NACION, Buenos Aires, Argentina, in Culture Section, November 26, 1997. "Peter Pran; Leading Modernist of the Late 90s: A Grand Master who is always young," by Marcelo Rizzo; partially an interview in connection with Peter Pran's participation in the International Buenos Aires Architecture Biennale 1997.

ARCADE, US West Coast architecture magazine, Winter 1997 issue "Altered Perceptions." Presentation of NBBJ projects by Peter Pran, Jonathan Ward, Jin Ah Park, Joey Myers, Jim Jonassen, Dan Meis, Michael Hallmark, Dorman Anderson, Rick Buckley.

L'ARCA PLUS, "80-Story Mixed-Use Tower," by Peter Pran, Jonathan Ward, Timothy Johnson, John Pangrazio, and Dorman Anderson of NBBJ, September 1997 special issue on *New International High-Rise Design*, Milan, Italy.

L'ARCA, "80-story Jakarta Mixed-Use Tower," by Peter Pran, Jonathan Ward, Timothy Johnson, Dorman Anderson, November 1996, Milan, Italy

SCANORAMA, SAS in-flight magazine, "The Man With the Plan: Peter Pran's International Architectural Designs," by Cecilie Holter, May 1996, published by SAS in Stockholm, Sweden.

PROJETO, "Architectural High Tech for Large Corporations: Work by Peter Pran," by Fumihiko Maki, November 1995, Sao Paolo, Brazil

L'ARCA, "South Point Tower, Miami, Florida," by Peter Pran, Timothy Johnson, Jonathan Ward, December 1995, Milan, Italy

L'ARCA, "New York City Police Academy," by Peter Pran, Timothy Johnson, September 1995, Milan, Italy

581 ARCHITECTS IN THE WORLD, Tokyo, Japan, December 1995. The fifty architects from the USA, including Peter Pran, were selected by Aaron Betsky.

THE GLOBE & MAIL, "A Tip of the Hat to a Top Idea," *Sightlines* column, by Adele Freedman, July 2, 1994, feature article on Peter Pran's design of the Tip Top Tailors Master Plan, First Prize winner, Toronto, Ontario, Canada

ARKITEKTNYTT, "Peter Pran in Norway," by Bente Sand, June 1996, Oslo, Norway. Published by Norwegian Architecture Association (including front cover).

CASABELLA, feature article by Kenneth Frampton on New York

Police Academy by Peter Pran of Ellerbe Becket and Michael Fieldman, and the New York State Psychiatric Institute by Peter Pran, Timothy Johnson, and Jill Lerner, Fall 1993

THE NEW YORK TIMES, "Arts and Leisure section" feature and cover article "Modernism and Morality in South Bronx: New York Police Academy" designed by Peter Pran, Design Principal, New York; written by Herbert Muschamp, Sunday, March 28, 1993

ARCHITECTURAL DESIGN, "Visions for the Future," feature article on "New York Police Academy" by Peter Pran and Michael Fieldman. Fall 1993.

THEORY AND EXPERIMENTATION, ed. Andreas Papadakis, book presenting work by 20 international leading architects, including Peter Pran. Academy Editions, London, 1992.

PROGRESSIVE ARCHITECTURE, October 1991 issue, "From coast to coast modernism's leading edge," feature article on the design work of Peter Pran, Carlos Zapata, and Mehrdad Yazdani. Article written by Editor Thomas Fisher.

ARCHITECTURAL RECORD, feature article "Modernism in Motion: New Executive Offices by Peter Pran and Carlos Zapata put an Accounting Firm on the Cutting Edge," written by Clifford A. Pearson on Deloitte & Touche Headquarters designed by Peter Pran and Carlos Zapata, May 1990 issue, New York.

Books

Architectural Monographs: No. 24, Peter Pran of Ellerbe Becket, Recent Work, with essays by Kenneth Frampton, Fumihiko Maki, Daniel Libeskind, John Gaunt and Peter Pran, Academy Editions, London, 1992

Theory and Experimentation, ed. Andreas Papadakis, presentation of work of the 20 most innovative architects internationally, Academy Editions, London, 1992

100 Years of Architecture in Chicago, Continuity of Structure and Form, co-authored by Oswald Grube, Peter Pran and Franz Schulze, Follett Publishing Co., 1976

Exhibitions
Exhibits at museums and galleries around the world

Jury Member and Critic
Columbia University, New York
Harvard University, Boston
Tulane University, New Orleans
Parson School of Design, New York
Pratt Institute, New York, International Seminar
Observation Member, National Accrediting Team reviewing Columbia University School of Architecture, 1988
One of three finalists for Dean of Architecture position, Pratt Institute, Spring 1991
Yale University, New Haven, Connecticut
Jury Member; University of Karlsruhe, Germany
Jury Member; on Jury for international architecture competition for New Art and Media Cultural Center (AKM), Karlsruhe, Germany
San Diego, California, AIA Annual Design Awards Jury
Iowa AIA State Chapter Annual Design Awards Jury
Portland AIA Chapter Annual Design Awards Jury
Seattle AIA Chapter AIA Annual Design Awards Jury
Virginia AIA State Chapter Annual Design Awards Jury
Washington DC AIA Chapter Annual Design Awards Jury
Los Angeles AIA Chapter Annual Design Awards Jury
NIAE, Paris Prize Jury (in New York)
Philadelphia AIA Chapter Annual Design Awards
Cleveland AIA Chapter Annual Design Awards
Eight Midwest States AIA Design Awards
Canadian Design Awards, for *The Canadian Architect*
Summer University, Würzburg, Germany (organized by Italian Universities, Milan, Italy)
Orange County, AIA Chapter Annual Design Awards Jury, California

Lectures
Technical University, Helsinki, Finland
University of Wisconsin, Milwaukee, Wisconsin
Ball State University, Indiana
Instituto Tecnologico y de Estudios Superiores de Monterrey, Mexico
Louisiana State University, Baton Rouge, Louisiana
FAMU/University of State of Florida, Tampa
University of Tennessee, Knoxville, Tennessee
Mississippi State University

NTH University, Trondheim, Norway
NAL Trondheim, Norway
NAL Bergen, Norway
NAL Stavanger, Norway
Walker Art Center, Minneapolis, Minnesota, 1988
University of Palermo, Sicily, Italy
Oslo Arkitekthögskole, Oslo, Norway
Catholic University, Washington DC
Iowa AIA State Convention, Des Moines, Iowa
Wichita AIA, Kansas, University of Kansas, Lawrence
Portland Chapter AIA Annual Convention, Portland, Oregon
Carnegie Mellon University, Pittsburgh, Pennsylvania
Seattle AIA Annual Convention at the University of Washington
Indonesian Architect Association, Jakarta, Indonesia
Kanto Gakuin University, Yokohama/Tokyo
NEOCON, Chicago
University of Kentucky
Wichita AIA, Kansas
University of Kansas, Lawrence
Virginia State AIA Convention, Richmond, Virginia
Kansas City AIA, Kansas City, Missouri
Montana State University, Montana
Royal Academy, Copenhagen, Denmark
University of Florida, Tampa, Florida
Asian Architect Association, Jakarta, Indonesia
Asian Architect Association, Kuala Lumpur, Malaysia
Indiana State AIA Annual Convention
University of Karlsruhe, Germany
University of Southern California, Los Angeles
Columbia University, New York City
North Dakota State University
University of Illinois, Urbana-Champaign
Woodbury University, Burbank, California
University of Washington, Seattle, together with Jonathan Ward
Urban Center Gallery, New York City
International Architecture Bienal at the Museo Nacional de Bellas Artes, Buenos Aires, Argentina
Council on Tall Buildings and Urban Habitat, Sao Paulo, Brasil

Symposia
New American Architecture at Technical University, Helsinki
New Chicago Architecture at Palazzo della Gran Guardia, Verona, Italy
New Directions in European Architecture at University of Rome, Italy
A Search for Meaning: Present Directions in Architecture.
International symposium in honour of Christian Norberg-Schulz's 60th birthday, at Grand Hotel, Oslo, Norway
The New Moderns, Royal Institute of British Architects, London, sponsored by the Academy Group and the Royal Academy of Arts
Design Awards Symposium of Los Angeles Chapter AIA, at Hollywood Building, Los Angeles (with Charles Gwathmey, Deborah Dietch, Adele Naude Santos, and Peter Pran)
Architecture in Arcadia, the Royal Academy of Arts, London
Theory & Experimentation, the Royal Academy of Arts, London
Modern Redux, Panel Discussion at New York University with Bill Lacy, John Hejduk, Peter Pran, Michael Sorkin, Douglas Davis
Asian Architect Association, Kuala Lumpur, Malaysia and Jakarta, Indonesia (with Kisho Kurukawa, Ken Yang, Rem Koolhaas, Charles Correa, and Peter Pran)
National AIA Convention, Chicago, 1993, and New Book Presentation by Thom Maine, Mack Scogin and Peter Pran
Symposium at Arkitekthöyskolen University with Christian Norberg-Schulz, Sverre Fehn, Peter Pran, Nils Mjaaland, Ketil Thorsen in Oslo, Norway
Make and Remake, ITESM, Monterrey, Mexico, with Michael Sorkin, Elias Zenghelis, Peter Pran, Marc Wigley, Enrico Miralles, and Andreas Papadakis
New York Police Academy, Panel Discussion with Kenneth Frampton, Peter Pran and Michael Fieldman at Columbia University Wood Auditorium. Sponsored by the Buell Center for the Study of American Architecture and Columbia University, plus the Architectural League, and Municipal Arts Society, New York
Contemporary Architecture Directions, at Orange County, AIA, California Symposium with Mark Mack, Michael Kosaleck and Peter Pran

TV Programme
Jahn Otto Johansen presented a 30-minute feature programme *Peter Pran and his Building Designs in New York* on Norwegian television, December 5, 1986

Recent Selected Writings by Peter Pran
"Altered Perceptions" in *Arcade Magazine*, December 1997, co-authored with Jonathan Ward, Jin Ah Park, and Joey Myers of NBBJ
"Urban Futures: An Innovative Modern Architecture for Tall

Buildings," in *Book Proceedings*, International Council on Tall Buildings and Urban Habitats, Sao Paulo, Brazil, October 1997.
Editorial News: "Catch the 5:05 from Jakarta," presenting Peter Pran's design for the Manggaria Transportation Centre, *Progressive Architecture*, December 1995
John Currie, Peter Pran, and Ron Turner: "Creating Places: Architecture as a Means to an Organization's Goals," in *Design Management Journal*, Volume 5, #1, Winter 1994
Stephen Perrella: "New York City Police Training Academy, by Peter Pran, Timothy Johnson and Michael Fieldman," in *Newsline*, May/Summer 1993, published by Columbia University Graduate School of Architecture, Planning and Preservation, New York City
Peter Pran - Recent Works with essays by Kenneth Frampton, Fumihiko Maki, Daniel Libeskind, John Gaunt and Peter Pran, Academy Editions, London, 1993
"The Architecture of the Southern Tip of Manhattan, New York," with presentation of Battery Park (low-rise) Cultural Center, inserted into the water, designed by Peter Pran and Carlos Zapata, *Metropolis Magazine*, New York, October 1991.

Recent Articles and Presentations on Peter Pran
Internet interview with Peter Pran, NBBJ, on internet in USA/internationally by Don Cornish on October 8, 1997
Editorial "Architects Compete for Telenor Headquarters." Interview with Scott Wyatt and Peter Pran of NBBJ in *Aftenposten* newspaper, September 30, 1997, Oslo, Norway
"Interview with Peter Pran," (about Telenor competition and his work) *Teknisk Ukeblad*, November 1997, Oslo, Norway
"Intense Competition for Telenor Project," in *AskerogBrerum Budshikke*, October 1997, Oslo, Norway
Ging Mata: "Judy's Towering Monuments" in *Lifestyle Asia* magazine, March 1997. Projects developed by Judith Duavit Vazquez and her company DUVAZ, including El Presidente in Manila, design by NBBJ - Peter Pran, Dorman Anderson, Jonathan Ward, Budy Djuanedi, Duncan Griffin, and Lor'Calma - Ed Calma
Jane Merkel, ed.: "The Future is Now." Article on the recent architecture of Peter Pran, Jonathan Ward and Timothy Johnson in New York City, *Oculus*, NYC/AIA Magazine, May 1996, Volume 58, #9
Nina Tjonasland: "In the Building Art's Top World Class," *Stavanger Aftenblad* newspaper, May 21, 1996, Norway.
Michael J. Crosbie: "Two Paths to Competitive Success," *Architectural Record*, September 1996
Joel Sanders: "Kontaminirte Modern." Review of innovative modern work including the New York Police Academy.in *Stadt Bauwelt* magazine, March 31, 1995, Berlin, Germany
Cecilie Holter: "New City Center to be designed by Peter Pran," in cultural section, *Aftenposten*, July 15, 1995, Oslo, Norway.
Christina Pletten: "Prophet in Another Country" Feature article in *Dagens Naeringsliv* newspaper, Saturday, August 19, 1995
Larry Wayne Richards: "Peter Pran: On Top For Tip Top - A Triumph for Modernism on Toronto's Lakefront," in *Competitions* magazine, Spring 1995, Louisville, Kentucky.
Editorial News: "Catch the 5:05 from Jakarta," article on Manggarai Transportation Center in *Progressive Architecture*, December 1995
Gregory Palermo, *Iowa Architect*, Awards Issue, Winter 1995, presenting annual design awards for AIA Iowa and AIA Central States (IA, MO, KS, OK, NE), for which Peter Pran was jury member
Jim Sleeper: "Mayor Shouldn't Cop Out on This Plan," on New York Police Academy, *Daily News* newspaper, June 16, 1994, New York
David W. Dunlap: "Reading the Giuliani Spending Blueprint." Presents Peter Pran as Design Principal, in collaboration with Michael Fieldman, Principal. *The New York Times*, June 12, 1994
Beth Kapusta, Herbert Enns, Kim Storey, Peter Pran: "Reflections on the 1994 Canadian Design Awards," *The Canadian Architect*, December 1994, Toronto, Canada.
Tip Top Tailor, Toronto, winning competition project, designed by Peter Pran and Tim Johnson, editorial presentation, *The Canadian Architect*, August 1994
Brad McKee: "American Architects in Asia," (Crystal Garden Apartment Tower), in *Architecture*, September 1994
Dennis Domer: "Nurturing Creativity in Architectural Education and Practice: An Interview with John Gaunt," in *The Structurist*, No. 33/34, 1993/94, University of Saskatchewan, Saskatoon, Canada
John Currie, Peter Pran, and Ron Turner: "Creating Places: Architecture as a Means to an Organization's Goals," in *Design Management Journal*, Vol. 5, #1, Winter 1994, Boston, MA.
Christopher Johnston: "AIA Celebrates 1993 Design Awards," AIA Cleveland Chapter, presenting the work of Jury Chairperson Peter Pran, in *Architecture*, January 1994
Mark A. Hewitt: "Rebuilding the Armature of Civic Art: The Bronx Police Academy," in *Competitions* magazine, Vol. 3, Spring 1993.

Stephen Perrella: "New York City Police Training Academy, by Peter Pran, Timothy Johnson and Michael Fieldman," in *Newsline*, May/Summer 1993, Columbia University Graduate School of Architecture, Planning and Preservation, New York City.

JONATHAN R. WARD

Education
Master of Architecture, Virginia Polytechnic Institute, Alexandria, VA
Bachelor of Arts in Architecture, University of Minnesota, Minneapolis, Minnesota
Urban Planning Studies, University of Nijmegen, Nijmegen, Netherlands

Awards
Korean Museum of Art in LA, International Competition, Honorable Mention, 1995
The Nolli Prize, University of Minnesota, 1992
Minnesota Concrete Institute Award, 1992

Publications
Seoul Dome, *L'Arca*, February 1998
"Altered Perceptions," *Arcade, the Journal for Architecture and Design in the Northwest*, Winter 1997
"Digital Worlds," *Architecture*, June 1997
Jakarta 80-storey Tower, "Towers & Skyscrapers," *L'Arca Plus*
Jakarta 80-storey Tower, *L'Arca*, December, 1996
Graha Kunigan, Rail Control Center, Manggarai Transportation Center, *World Architecture*, May 1996
" Peter Pran: Design Technology," Karet Office Tower, Graha Kunigan, 80-storey Tower, *New Architecture*, I, Papadakis, London 1997
Oculus, May 1996
TNB Tower, *L'Arca*, May 1996
Portofino Apartment Tower, *L'Arca*, December 1995
Manggarai Integrated Transportation Terminal, *Progressive Architecture*, December 1995
Karet Office Tower, *Projecto*, October 1995
Korean Museum of Art in LA, *Plus*, May 1995
Masters Thesis, *Washington City Paper*, Vol. 14, No. 44, Nov. 4-10, 1994

Teaching
Assistant Professor, University of Washington, Winter, 1998
Visiting Lecturer, University of Washington, Winter, 1997
Visiting Professor & Lecturer, University of Kansas, Fall 1997
Design Critic, Catholic University, 1994

Exhibitions
Masters Thesis, *Visions of Home Exhibit at the National Building Museum*, Washington, DC, Fall 1994-Spring 1995 (an exhibit of Washington architects' progressive housing projects)
El Presidente

Selected buildings and projects
Dayton Cultural & Community Center, Dayton, OH. Senior Designer
El Presidente, Makati, Philippines. Senior Project Designer
International Business Center, Daewoo Corporation, Korea. Senior Project Designer
Jakarta Mixed-Use Tower, Jakarta, Indonesia. Senior Project Designer
Manggarai Integrated Transportation Terminal, Jakarta, Indonesia. Senior Project Designer
Mok-Dong Commercial Complex, Seoul, Korea. Project Designer
Reebok International Ltd., Stoughton, Massachusetts, Corporate headquarters on 42-acre campus, approximately 460,000 square feet. Lead Senior Project Designer
Seoul Dome, Seoul, Korea. Winner of international design competition. Competition Senior Project Designer
Kwun Tong Town Center, Hong Kong, People's Republic of China. Senior Project Designer
Telenor, Oslo, Norway. Senior Designer
King Fahd Children's Cancer Center, Riyadh, Saudi Arabia. Project Designer
Wyoming Valley Medical Center, Wilkes Barre, PA. Project Designer
Sperbank, Moscow, Russia (opened summer 1995). Senior Project Designer
BCC Trade Center, Moscow, Russia. Project Designer
The Franke Home, Charleston, South Carolina. Design development and construction documents for nursing home.
Drug Enforcement Agency Training Facility, Fairfax, Virginia. Junior designer on new training facility for the DEA.

World Bank, Washington D.C. Work on a design and video for interior design of the World Bank's Africa Development Center.
Texas Children's Cancer Center, Houston, Texas. Work on design of new interior. Project Designer
Resort Hotel, Hurghada, Egypt. Proposal for a new ocean-front, 400-room hotel and casino. Project Designer
University of Chicago Natatorium, Chicago, Illinois. Schematic design. Project Designer
East Texas Medical Center, Tyler, Texas. Work on conceptual design through design development. Project Designer
Curitiba Arena and Mixed-Use Project, Curitiba, Brazil. Lead Project Designer
Mozadi Office Building, Jakarta, Indonesia. Designer during conceptual and schematic phase
SBS Broadcasting Center Competition, Seoul, Korea. Lead Project Designer
Komplex Kirab Remadja, Jakarta, Indonesia. Project Designer
TNB Tower Competition, Kuala Lumpur, Malaysia. Senior Project Designer
Graha Kuningan, Jakarta, Indonesia. Conceptual Senior Designer
Manggarai Integrated Transportation Terminal + New Jakarta City Center, Jakarta, Indonesia. Senior Project Designer
Karet Office Tower, Jakarta, Indonesia. Lead Project Designer
Portofino Apartment Tower, Miami, Florida. Project Designer
Jackson Memorial Hospital, Miami, Florida. Competition for a new psychiatric facility for the hospital. Lead Project Designer
Korea-Russia Trade Center, Moscow, Russia. Lead Project Designer
NTCTA Rail Control Center, New York, NY.
This 133,000 sq.ft building will be the control centre for all subway movement in the city of New York. Designer
NYCTA Church Avenue Station, New York, NY. Renovation of existing subway station in Brooklyn. Computer visualization and renderings.
Ellerbe Becket, New York, NY. Coordinated and produced graphic design for 12 high-end project posters as part of the renovation of the New York office. Also designed and built poster frames. Graphic Designer
La Plaza Cultural, New York, New York
A garden/park in the Lower East Side of Manhattan which is being renovated and returned to the community. Created an overall master plan for the site, approximately one-half a city blocks. Co-designer
Velona Art Gallery; Philadelphia, PA. An in-fill one space gallery, 500 sq.ft with rotating collection. Designer, computer renderings
Somali Residence, Jakarta, Indonesia. Designer, computer renderings
Korean Museum of Art and Cultural Center, Los Angeles, CA International competition, 1,600 entrants worldwide, received Honorable Mention and cash prize. Co-designer

TIMOTHY J. JOHNSON

Education
Master of Science, Advanced Architectural Design, Columbia University, New York City, NY, USA
Bachelor of Architecture, School of Architecture and Landscape Architecture, University of Minnesota

Professional Experience
Principal ARC-NYC, 1996-present
Design Director, Ellerbe Becket, New York, 1990-96
Project Designer, Ellerbe Becket, Minneapolis, 1988-90

Teaching/Lectures
Columbia University, Graduate School of Architecture, Planning, and Preservation, New York, NY
Clemson University, Urban Studies, Genova, Italy
University of Kansas, School of Architecture, Lawrence, Kansas

Affiliation
American Institute of Architects

Registration
New York State

Design Prizes/Awards
Civic Architecture New York, 1995
Modern Healthcare, American Institute of Architects Design Award, 1995
Progressive Architecture "Young Architects" Award, 1993
American Institute of Architects, New York Chapter, Design Award, 1992
Skidmore, Owings & Merrill Foundation, Travelling Fellowship, 1992

William F. Kinne Travelling Fellowship, 1992
CSI Technology Award, 1992
SPQR Rome Prize, 1990

Project Experience

Corporate Office
Menara PSP, Jakarta, Indonesia
McDonald's Indonesia, Corporate Headquarters, Jakarta
Menara Bank Global, Jakarta, Indonesia
Graha Bank Baja, Jakarta, Indonesia
Gambir Telecommunications Tower, Jakarta, Indonesia
Wisma INTUK, Jakarta, Indonesia
Sudirman 63, Jakarta, Indonesia
Warung Buncit Tower, Jakarta, Indonesia
Graha Kuningan, Jakarta, Indonesia
Karet Office Tower, Jakarta, Indonesia
Jakarta Mixed-Use Tower, Jakarta, Indonesia
Tenaga Nasional Berhad Office Building, Kuala Lumpur, Malaysia
Mozadi Intelligent Office Building, Jakarta, Indonesia
Elihu M. Harris State Office Building, Oakland, California
Corporate Headquarters, Jeddah, Saudi Arabia
Bin-Laden Headquarters, Jeddah, Saudi Arabia
CN/Royal Trust Office Building, Toronto, Ontario, Canada
LaSalle Plaza, Minneapolis, Minnesota
Teleport Town Office Tower, Tokyo, Japan

International
Karawang Mixed-Use, Karawang-Barat, Indonesia
Komplek Kirab Remaja, Jakarta, Indonesia
New Jakarta City Center, Jakarta, Indonesia
Manggarai Integrated Transportation Terminal, Jakarta, Indonesia
Daniprisma Plaza, Jakarta, Indonesia
Flameco Soccer Stadium, Rio de Janeiro, Brazil
Curitiba Stadium and Mixed-Use, Curitiba, Brazil
Tip-Top Tailors Master Plan, Toronto, Ontario, Canada
Banco Popular, Ibarra, Ecuador
KIA Motors Automobile Pavilion, Taejon, Korea
De Centrale Lokatie, The Hague, Netherlands
Washington Hotel, Hiroshima, Japan

Educational
New York City Police Academy, New York, NY
New Academic Buildings, State University of New York, Binghamton, NY
New York City Transit Rail Control Center, New York, NY
Minneapolis Energy Corporation Emissions Tower, Minneapolis, Minnesota

Research/Medical
New York State Psychiatric Institute, New York, NY
Columbia University Center for Disease Prvention, New York, NY
Rikshospitalet, Oslo, Norway

Residential
Apartment PSP, Jakarta, Inonesia
Thee Residence, Jakarta, Indonesia
Sumali Residence, Jakarta, Indonesia
Portofino South Point Tower, Miami Beach, Florida

Interiors
PT Indoverse Securities, Jakarta, Indonesia
Citrus Restaurant, Jakarta, Indonesia
Bank Global, Banking Hall and Corporate Headquarters, Jakarta, Indonesia
Bank Media, Banking Hall and Corporate Headquarters, Jakarta, Indonesia
PT Duta Anggada Realty Headquarters, Jakarta, Indonesia
PT Great Giant Pineapple Corporate Headquarters, Jakarta, Indonesia
Jakarta Steel Group Corporate Headquarters, Jakarta, Indonesia
PT Pacific MetroRealty Corporate Headquarters, Jakarta, Indonesia
Bank Bahari, Banking Hall and Executive Offices, Jakarta, Indonesia

PAUL QUINN DAVIS

Education
Bachelor, University of Minnesota

Professional Positions
Senior Project Designer, NBBJ Sports & Entertainment, LA
Project Designer, Ellerbe Becket Inc., Minneapolis (1986-96)
Co-founder Logic Error, Artist Collaborative, Minneapolis, Minnesota 1993-

Co-founder, Unfam Art, Artist Collaborative, St. Paul, Minnesota, 1992
Founder, Ellwood Productions, Entertainment Venue, Minneapolis, MN, 1990

Awards
Young Architect Design Award, *Progressive Architecture*, 1993
Computer Delineation Award, 1st place, Logic Error, *Architectural Record*, 1996
Computer Graphics Award, 1st place, Logic Error, *Fast Electronic*, 1995
Design Award, New York Police Academy, Bronx, New York, AIA, 1992
Design Award, NYTT Rikshospitalet, Oslo, Norway, AIA, 1991
Thesis award, 1st place, *Ground Zero, Postnuclear Nightclub*, University of Minnesota, Cala, 1990
Design Award, 1st place, "The Dream," *Paper Architecture*, MSAIA 1989
Design Award, 1st place, *Kinder Kastle*, St. Paul Ice Castle Competition, 1984

Selected buildings and projects

Corporate, Commercial, International
Kingdom Trade Center, 65-storey Office Tower, Riyadh, Saudi Arabia, 1996
Grahan Kuningan, 52-storey Office Tower, Jakarta, Indonesia, 1995-96
General Mills Leadership Center, Minneapolis, Minnesota, 1994
Hoffman Laroche Corp. HQ, Office Tower (competition), Nutley, New Jersey, 1994
De Centrale in Den Haag, Office Tower, The Hague, Netherlands, 1992
Nikken Fukuoka Airport (competition), Fukuoka, Japan, 1991
Banco Popular, Bank, Quito, Ecuador, 1990
CN/Labatts Corp. HQ Office Tower (competition), Toronto, Canada, 1990
Sato Kogyo Corp. HQ, Office Tower (competition), Tokyo, Japan, 1990
Bin Laden Corp. HQ, Office Tower, Jeddah, Saudi Arabia, 1990
MPLS Energy Center, Boiler Stack, Urban Sculpture, Minneapolis, Minnesota, 1990
Washington Hotel (competition), Hiroshima, Japan, 1989
CN/Royal Trust Corp. HQ, Office Tower, Toronto, Canada, 1989
Javitz Center, Trade Mart/Hotel (competition), New York, NY, 1989

Government
U. S. Courthouse (competition), Minneapolis, MN, 1993
U. S. Courthouse (competition, 1st place), Missouri, 1992
Federal Triangle (competition, 1st place), Washington DC, 1989

Sports, Entertainment, Retail
Cincinnati Bengals Football Stadium, Cincinnati, Ohio, 1997-98
Atlanta Hawks Basketball Arena (proposal), Atlanta, Georgia, 1996
Sapporo Dome, Soccer Stadium (competition), Sapporo, Japan, 1996
Performance, Computer Generated Environment, *Glam Slam*, Minneapolis, Minnesota, 1994
Performance, Computer Generated Environment, *1st Ave.*, Minneapolis, Minnesota, 1994
Carole Bruns Fashion Boutique, Minneapolis, Minnesota, 1994
Sony Project 2000, Entertainment Prototype, multiple locations, *Earth*, 1993
Jean Charles Clothing Store, Minneapolis, Minnesota, 1993
University of Chicago, Natatorium/Gymnasium, Chicago, Illinois, 1992
KIA Automotive Pavilion, Taejon Expo, Seoul, Korea, 1990

Academic
Iowa State University, Science and Technology, Des Moines, Iowa, 1995
Carlson School of Management, Business School, Minneapolis, Minnesota, 1994
Cleveland State University, Business School, Cleveland, Ohio, 1994
New York Police Academy (competition, 1st place), Bronx, New York, 1992
Stanford University, Cancer Research Facility (competition), Palo Alto, California, 1992

Medical, Laboratory
East Texas Medical Center, M.O.B., Tyler, Texas, 1991
St. Luke's Methodist Hospital, Diagnostic Tower/MRI, Cedar Rapids, Iowa, 1990-91
NYTT Rikshospitalet, M.O.B. (competition, 1st place), Oslo, Norway, 1990

Northwestern Memorial Hospital (competition, 1st place), Chicago, Illinois, 1990
Cedar Sinai Hospital (competition), Los Angeles, California, 1990
East Tennesee Baptist Hospital (competition), M.O.B., Knoxville, Tennesee, 1989
Methodist Medical Center, Perinatal/Critical Care, Peoria, Illinois, 1989
Ridgeview Medical Center, Labor Delivery Suite, Waconia, Minnesota, 1989
Mayo Clinic, Charleton Building, Diagnostic Facility, Rochester, Minnesota, 1986-87

Exhibits
Hutchinson Technologies/Installation, Logic Error, Hutchinson, Minnesota, 1995
NYC/AIA Design Awards Exhibit, New York, NY, 1992
NYC/AIA Design Awards Exhibit, New York, NY, 1991
100-year Anniversary Exhibit, *Contemporary Architectural Drawing*, Columbia University, 1991
Cathedral Hill Art Exhibition, Unfam Art, St. Paul, MN, 1989

Lectures
Visiting Critic, Fall Semester, University of Kansas, 1997
Joey Myers/Paul Davis, University of Southern California, 1997
Paul Davis/Visual Communication, University of Minnesota, 1990-1996
Davis/Johnson/Pran of Ellerbe Becket, University of Kansas, 1995

Publications

Journals
World Architecture, "Inside Ellerbe Becket" (Graha Kuningan, cover), Carlson School of Management, Iowa State University, May 1996
Architectural Record, Computer Delineation Award (Logic Error), June, 1995
L'Arca, New York Police Academy, October, 1995
Architecture Minnesota, "On the Boards," (Logic Error), June 1994.
Architectural Design, "Visions for the Future," New York Police Academy, Academy Group Ltd, London, 1993.
Progressive Architecture, Young Architects Award Issue, July 1993
The New York Times, "Modernism and Morality in the South Bronz," (New York Police Academy), Sunday, March 28, 1993.
Architecture (New York Police Academy, February, 1993.
Architectural Record (New York Police Academy, February, 1993.
Progressive Architecture (New York Police Academy), January 1993
Ambiente. "Die Utopie der Stadt," (KIA Automotive Pavilion), Thomsen, September 1992.
Progressive Architecture, "Hospitals made Simple," (St. Luke's Diagnostic Tower), Arcidi, March 1992
Progressive Architecture, "Ellerbe Becket explores from Coast to Coast Modernism's Leading Edge," (NYTT Tikshospitalet, Banco Popular, Bin Laden Corporate HQ, Fisher, October 1991
Architectural Design, "The New Modern Aesthetic" (Bin Laden Corporate HQ, CN/Labatts Corporate HQ), Academy Group Ltd., July 1990.
Architecture Minnesota, "Interpreting Dreams," (Minneapolis Energy Center), Knox, July 1990.
Architecture Minnesota, MSAIA Paper Architecture Awards Issue, "The Dream," July, 1989.

Books
Virtual Dimension (Logic Error), Princeton Assoc. Press, Beckman, 1998
Theory + Experimentation, ed. A. Papadakis, Academy Editions, London 1993.
Architectural Monographs No. 24, *Peter Pran of Ellerbe Becket, Recent Works*, Academy Editions, London 1992
Contemporary Architectural Drawings of Avery Library and Art Collection (NYTT Rikshospitalet), Columbia University, New York, Parks, 1991.

Technology
Development of IBM'S architectural engineering software (AES). a computer modelling tool used in the design process of architecture, the communication of ideas to the client and the marketing of new jobs.